I am the Specialist of the Strange

Dakota Frandsen

© 2024 Dakota Frandsen
"I am the Specialist of the Strange"
Published by Bald and Bonkers Network LLC
ISBN/SKU: 979-8-8693-3238-7, 979-8-3304-8501-7, 979-8-3304-8500-0
All rights reserved. No part of this publication may be reproduced, distributed, or transmitted in any form or by any means, including photocopying, recording, or other electronic or mechanical methods, without the prior written permission of the publisher, except in the case of brief quotations embodied in critical reviews or certain other noncommercial uses permitted by copyright law.
Images labeled as "AI Depictions" were generated using Ideogram.ai for illustrative purposes only and may not necessarily guarantee accurate depictions of events described

I AM THE SPECIALIST OF THE STRANGE

This book is dedicated to my Starlight Angel...
My beacon of hope, my eternal flame, my beloved wife.
To you, I pledge my destiny, the muse of my every heartbeat, the radiance in my soul, the fire piercing through the shadows. Your essence is a fantasy made flesh, a dream bestowed upon the fortunate few. In your dreams, may you feel my presence; upon waking, may you sense my thoughts.
Through the night, I embrace you, envisioning the brighter days that await us. "I love you" is but a humble tribute to the force you are in my life, yet these words scarcely capture the breadth of my adoration. Your divine aura uplifts me; the sweetness of your kiss deepens with time, binding me ever tighter to you. Daily, I strive to convey my love, and though it may require a Herculean effort for you to perceive your own splendor as I do, I lay the foundation for a legacy that will etch our tale into the annals of eternity, for my love transcends both time and space.

Contents

Dedication   v

1   A Letter From the Author   1
2   Before I Was "Dakota"   7
3   Early Life as "Dakota"   21
4   Growing Up and Taking Aim   35
5   Becoming the Man   61
6   Officially an Adult   83
7   Becoming the Specialist of the Strange   135
8   This Was War   161
9   Extraterrestrial Revelations   195
10   Reflections of the Specialist   257

Links for More Information   265
About the Author   267

1

A Letter From the Author

Dear Reader,

    I don't know what made you pick up this book or what's going on in your life at this time. Honestly, I have wondered why I even published it. It was meant to reveal some of the darkest secrets I had ever kept. It was stuff that I was quite literally too afraid to share until now. I've tried to share my own story before, in other ways: take those "Dear Kota" letters and make them into more. I wanted to look back at the days that shaped who we are, share personal journals and findings from years of research.

    But between weird technical glitches and my own reaction to the stress of it all, I lost it all more times than I could count. Maybe someday I'll do a fuller release, if I can ever figure out how to keep it all in one piece.

Something—or someone—deleted everything they could reach. Fortunately, I had backups to rescue what I could. But no sooner would I sit down to relate more about my strange life than something yanked me off on another adventure. Some people really think the title I carry, "Specialist of the Strange," is a bit of pretentiousness I dreamt up, but it was actually coined as a joke that got out of hand from a good friend that spiraled into something much bigger.

Dear Kota:
Time to Fess up
Cover

Life goes in funny ways, right?

Enough about that. What matters now is why you're holding this book and what I need to warn you about before you dive in.

Dakota before an Interview

My name is Dakota Frandsen, and my life has been packed with things most people would call "supernatural." There are plenty of days I wish it wasn't, times I've wished I could be "normal." Then again, when I see what society calls "normal" these days, I'd rather stick with the unknown. They called me the "Specialist of the Strange" because dealing with forces beyond this world had become second skin to me. I'd fought ghosts, hunted monsters, fought gods, and even had some pretty wild encounters with beings from other worlds. I know it sounds far-fetched, and I don't blame you if you're skeptical. Honestly, even with evidence of some of these experiences, I sometimes question my own sanity. It's part of why the name of my company, "Bald and Bonkers," stuck-but that's a story for another day.

I'm including this note as a heads-up. Aside from censoring a few details to protect people's privacy, I'm not holding anything back.

Some of what you'll read might break your heart, and some might haunt your nights like it did mine. But if I am to truly understand the realities of the world out there, or how those events shaped me into the person I am today, I am compelled to share everything-the good, the bad, the joy, the pain, the dreams, and the nightmare.

As I sifted through the repressed memories of this life and others, a lot came up-even I wasn't ready for.

Maybe this warning seems dramatic, but I've decided to publish my journals as they were written, with minimal edits except for the privacy of others. These records are raw, unfiltered, and written as they came to me in the moment.

I have done my best to retain details as accurately as possible, but the mind is a fragile thing. I've been fortunate in working with some mentors that helped me see through the fog and understand what I went through. A lot of the extraterrestrial species names, worlds, and more are based on what they taught me, as I have always felt the generic New Age terms don't do justice to the reality that I have seen.

This isn't about copying anyone's story. These are my experiences, though some do overlap with others. People have called me the "real-life Dean Winchester" after hearing some of my adventures. Others have tried to link me to secret societies, probably because I've had the chance to work on major projects in books, movies, TV, and even scientific expeditions.

There've been plenty of conspiracy theories out there claiming I'm someone else—some other figure with a similar story—and calling me a fraud. It's annoying, but I've learned to deal with it.

Honestly, it's part of the reason I just really like working alone. Religious overtones, ego, and drama are just a bunch of crap I've managed to edit out of my life. What happened in 2024 really drove that home-just how far I'd strayed from my path. But it's never too late to course-correct. Trust me or don't believe me-that is your prerogative-but this is my story. I hope, in some measure, you find something helpful in it. Let me warn you beforehand-this journey connects me to some of the darkest events in history. Even mentioning some of these things has placed my friends and family in danger.

Consider yourself warned... But beyond that, I hope these entries help you understand how my mind works. It has been lonely; I do know others out there are having their own struggles. Though our stories might be different, the key to making it through will be shared experiences through which new ideas and solutions come from our very own stories. Maybe that is why the powers that be keep us so divided. But we have the power to take control. It's sitting around, waiting for someone else to save us, that let the corrupt take over in the first place. So here's my contribution.

With Love,

Dakota Frandsen

Specialist of the Strange / Intergalatic Gigolo

CEO of the Bald and Bonkers Network LLC

Bald and Bonkers Network LLC

Logo

2

Before I Was "Dakota"

Dates Undetermined - Estimated Earth Time 1920 – 1995

Location: Planet Taalihara

As a teenager transitioning into adulthood, I was inducted into the Taalihara military forces. My rank was low, primarily involving patrol duties and occasional espionage to monitor potential rebel factions. The Taal Shiar, believed to be humanoid extraterrestrials, allegedly assisted the Third Reich during World War II. During a briefing, it was revealed that Maria Orsic

AI Depiction of German Soldiers in Antartica

received materials through telepathic communications under false pretenses, leading to the creation of alleged Nazi UFOs, sophisticated weaponry, and secret alliances forged just before 1930. By the 1940s, we retreated to what I believe was Antarctica before leaving Earth and returning to our home world.

My time with the Nazis triggered a sense of doubt about the mission and the pursuit of power. I was tasked with monitoring humans and potentially infiltrating Adolf Hitler's security detail. I killed men, women, and children, justifying these actions as consequences of war. I viewed humans as weak, inferior, and easily manipulated. Despite my doubts, I believed I was serving a proper cause.

One night, back on Taalihara, I witnessed a Draconian, likely a Ciakharr royal, cornering three children with the intent to kill. I opened fire with a plasma-based rifle, likely injuring but not stopping the creature. I shouted for the children to run, directing them to a nearby escape pod—a sleek metal craft capable of carrying ten people plus supplies.

AI Depiction of Battle with Draconian

As we boarded the escape pod, the Draconian pursued us, attempting to bite the children. I fought back with the rifle, making little progress. The children's screams prompted the realization that I had to kill the Draconian to ensure our escape. The creature slammed its fists into the craft, shaking everything and everyone. I shouted for an override to bypass security protocols preventing takeoff due to an obstruction. Grabbing the creature's horns, I twisted its neck, aiming for what I believed to be a weak spot. The craft took off with the creature stuck in the door. As its neck cracked, the Draconian's eyes shifted from a rampaging reptile to a human expression, seemingly thanking me for ending its life.

I sent a distress call to the Federation, fearing retaliation and doubting acceptance due to my affiliation with the Taal Shiar (Renegade Pleiadian Group). A woman responded, directing me to an outpost to intercept the children and get them to safety. She offered me refuge, which I hesitantly accepted, asking for time to return to Taalihara to rescue my family. The woman understood, warning me that news was spreading about my rogue actions.

I returned home to find a mix of panic and confrontation. Some family members believed me, while others followed the official narrative. My mother, leading the opposition, accused me of endangering the family by saving the children. My sister was visibly torn, and my father eventually quieted everyone, acknowledging my difficult choice. He urged me to leave for the safety of all. The look in his eyes broke my heart, but it seemed he and I had the closest relationship our of everyone else; a bond that would be tended to in another life... if I'm understanding how it all unfolded.

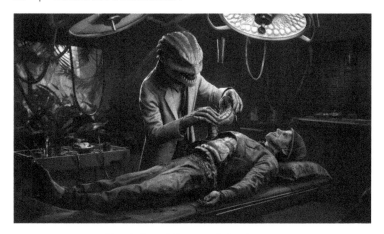

AI Depiction of Elaryon Being Tortured

Before I could properly escape, I was intercepted and knocked unconscious. When I awoke, I found myself bound to a table and my torso sliced open from the base of my neck to just above my crotch. A draconian scientist digging its scaled hands into my guts, it realized I was awake. It's language was similar to that of large iguanas and the recreations of a Tyrannosaurus call. The pitch and melody tingle at my spine just thinking about it. Once the being realized I was awake, it took great pleasure in torturing me; squeezing my lungs with its claws so I would be unable to scream in pain. My condition was far too compromised for any internal systems to properly function, but I could tell my captor was singing as it dug into my flesh.

I was only let go when the sound of a distant explosion rang through the facility. The sound reverberations told me the building was metal, possibly in a tropical environment somewhere. I watched as my torturer looked in the direction of the explosion, angered at being disrupted, and turning away. It simply left me there, sliced open like an animal in a butcher shop, barely holding on for dear life. I could hear a voice, possibly some kind of radio transmission, whispering for me to hold on as help was on the way. I could hear the commotion, my vision blurring as I held on for as long as I could, but the second I saw a man with a light blue uniform found me I knew I was saved. I couldn't help but let go in the moment, I was just happy to see someone human.

Returning to the Federation outpost, I was given time to process the ordeal. My tasks alternated between field medic/scientist and espionage, thanks to my Taal Shiar training. I also participated in the Starseed program, part of the Federation's envoy efforts.

Dates Undetermined

Location: Galactic Federation of Worlds Outposts

During my tenure with the Federation, I married a T'Ashkeru woman named Iveena, who hailed from Nyan, a planet near Sirius B. She left her home to join the Galactic Federation of Worlds (GFW) due to the growing influence of the Nebu. We quickly bonded over our shared backgrounds and discovered that our families had likely known each other through work-related activities.

Early AI Recreation of "Iveena"

Iveena was taller than most women from her world, standing nearly six feet tall. She had long blonde hair, prominent cheekbones, and a pointed chin. Her blonde hair and hypnotic blue eyes made her almost resemble a tall Asian woman. Certain aspects made her resemble a Japanaese manga character.

We both enlisted in the envoy program, sometimes sharing deployments and other times alternating duties. I frequently checked in on Iveena during her envoy deployment on Earth to ensure she was okay and well-treated. I remember reaching out to her during moments of distress, honoring our promise to always watch over each other.

A significant incident motivated my vigilance. While on a scientific expedition, the facility where Iveena and I worked was ambushed by amphibious beings, possibly Ciakharr hybrid experiments. I was in another part of the facility when the attack occurred. Though I managed to reach safety, Iveena was injured, her abdomen sliced open. Miraculously, the creature did not harm our unborn child. We were trying to start a family and came perilously close to losing our oldest daughter. Upon returning to the mothership, I learned of Iveena's injury. A colleague informed me that they had saved both her and the baby, but I needed to get to her immediately.

Upon hearing the news, I rushed to her side, nearly breaking through doors and smashing access panels in my haste. Iveena was the reason I enlisted; I had fallen in love with her, perhaps having known her in previous lifetimes. We were so close to starting a family, and the thought of losing it all was unbearable. When I found her, she was emerging from a medical pod that had restored her physical condition. I hurried over, embraced her tightly, and apologized for not being there. Though she returned the hug, her grip was weak—something was still wrong.

Iveena asked about the baby, and I assured her that our daughter had been saved and transferred to an incubation unit for proper development. While the medical technology had healed her physical wounds without leaving scars, the mental toll was beyond any machine's capability. Iveena felt abandoned during her and the baby's time of need. A close friend had ensured her safety and supported us, but the only true relief for her was an upcoming envoy deployment. She needed time away from the war and from us to think. Despite the heartbreak, I had to let her go, leaving me to raise our daughter with the

AI Depiction of Elaryon and Iveena

GFW's schooling systems until Iveena returned and I went on my own deployment.

The complexities of time travel make establishing this timeline challenging.

Estimated Earth Time: Somewhere late 1980s to early 1990s

Locations: Galactic Federation - (Possibly) The Excelsior - The Last Rescue

I recall one final rescue mission before my latest envoy deployment. Our team quickly assembled on a small craft that cloaked itself as we descended from a mothership in Earth's orbit.

We flew swiftly towards an area south of the Great Lakes, likely Indiana. Our ship hovered above a white colonial-style house. I and another male operative disembarked, cloaked and undetectable by radar systems.

The house was two stories tall, and the setting suggested the mission took place in the late 80s to early 90s. Two tall Greys emerged, carrying a small child—a girl no older than three, with brown hair and a bright red pajama dress, possibly a Christmas gift. One Grey ran its finger over the girl's body, even under her clothes. I was ready to intervene, but my colleague's hand on my shoulder reminded me to stay calm.

Our camouflage technology responded to our intentions, and losing control could have compromised the mission. Though we were well-trained, our individual issues sometimes affected our emotional states. It was crucial to check each other during operations to ensure success. Nothing angered us more than seeing an innocent child harmed.

We couldn't attack the Greys on the street without attracting too much attention and violating jurisdiction. Our mission was to trace their ship, gain access to their records, and rescue more children.

The Greys revealed their ship, allowing us to tag its signature and track it as it left Earth. Outside the planet's atmosphere, we ambushed their vessel, nearly killing the Greys in the process. We rescued the girl and recalibrated her implant to our channels. She was part of the envoy program, targeted by the Greys for experimentation, aimed at corrupting starseeds from within—a Trojan horse strategy.

We took the child on a joyride to calm her before wiping her memory and returning her home. Reflecting on the mission aboard the Excelsior, I was approached by ~~censored~~—a tall, blonde man with Nordic features, whom I regarded as both a brother-in-arms and a leader. Ahel Pleiadian, one of many groups the Taal Shiar almost carried a prejudice towards. Off-duty, he was laid-back and caring, with a talent for singing. He frequently visited with a young Earth girl, an envoy preparing for a grand revelation. She was his like his sister, ~~censored~~, and his motivation.

AI Depictions of Fellow GFW Soldiers Reflecting on the Mission Above Earth

~~censored~~ asked for my thoughts. I expressed concern for the young girl we had rescued. ~~censored~~ reassured me, chuckling, that I would see her again. He placed three fingers in a triangle against my forehead, preparing to suppress my memories of galactic involvement for the envoy transition. I understood the process but insisted on remembering the child and others we had saved, as it was my reason for joining the Federation. ~~censored~~ grinned and said, "Just remember the moose," before winking.

Estimated Earth Time: Somewhere before 1996

Location: Galactic Federation - Envoy Program Stasis Bay

There were conversations, more accurately briefings, detailing an upcoming envoy deployment. My wife was present, both as emotional support and to assist with any last-minute details. We had a transition period to help her readjust to intergalactic life and for me to tie up any loose ends. During most of the session, I felt only half-listening, preoccupied with thoughts of my wife and our discussions about starting a family.

Another individual, resembling a military recruiter, was also there. He had darker skin, almost black hair, and wore a dark gray uniform. He looked human, with a skinny and somewhat elongated face. His role was to address any concerns I had about the envoy assignment.

Key points discussed included:

- The body I was to inhabit had a strong predisposition to what humans called "psychic abilities," attributed to a predominant bloodline.

- These "abilities" would initially be activated by trauma and then occur at random times.

- One of my mission objectives was to understand how people could fall so easily under abusive and tyrannical rule.

- Another objective was to serve as a "warrior" on Earth, though not enlisted with any military or government body in an official capacity.

- Given our desire to start a family, the timing of operations on Earth seemed favorable.

- Many humanoid civilizations encouraged interplanetary relationships, a common practice intended to promote diplomatic cooperation and help future generations thrive in their environment.

- The timing referred to Earth entering its first stages of becoming an interplanetary society, transitioning from space travel being reserved for elites and those caught in trafficking operations.

- The first steps of the great introduction, when the most human-looking extraterrestrials would be permitted to show themselves publicly, was allegedly set for 2025.

- My new body would be monitored closely by the GFW and likely by Greys associated with the Ciakharr.

- Other family members on my Earth body's paternal side had reported possible abductions by Greys, likely for hybridization.

- People on my maternal side had shared details of UFO sightings, possibly connected to nearby military bases.

Once the necessary contracts were signed, there was a brief period for me to say my goodbyes. My wife and the recruiter were present when I was taken to a metallic white stasis pod. The pod had displays on the side, likely to monitor my vitals, and a glass opening. As my body was connected to the machine and a breathing apparatus attached to my face, I remember slowly drifting into unconsciousness as a cool blue liquid filled the pod. I saw my wife's tears and felt the hurt in her heart. I started to cry too, but my tears quickly merged with the gel surrounding me. The last thing I remember is saying, "I love you," as I rested my hand against the glass. My wife pressed her hand against the glass, aligning it with mine, as I blacked out.

3

Early Life as "Dakota"

Date(s): January 18-19, 1996

Location: Earth - Twin Falls, Idaho - Magic Valley Regional Medical Center

Shortly after losing consciousness, I experienced a rapid flash of various images and events, as if I was receiving a download of memories from countless lifetimes played at super speed. These memories didn't feel like personal experiences but rather as if they were being received. Some of the events seemed to be from the future.

Dakota Frandsen - 2 Months Old

© *Shannon Malone*

The more recent memories were easier to identify through old family photos, including dates my parents and grandparents went on, and possible histories of abuse discussed in conversations about estranged family members.

Older memories are more speculative. These included a possible child sacrifice, being rounded up by German soldiers, and potential experimentation by Greys.

The "download" (for lack of better word) ended with a bright flash of light, likely signifying my birth. I remember brief snippets of the delivery room with pale blue tiles and blinding light. I was born on January 19, 1996, at about 5:30 pm Mountain Time via emergency C-section due to postpartum hemorrhaging. I was my mother's first child, born at 12 lbs 4 oz, already holding my head up. Aside from mild pneumonia, I was a healthy child, just larger than expected.

Date: November, 1997 estimated

Location: Earth - United States - Idaho

My first "psychic" episode

This is a story I have only fragments of, but it is one my aunts (my father's sisters) frequently recounted. My parents were never married, so I underwent shared custody arrangements. While staying with my father and stepmother, I approached my stepmother, placed my hand over her stomach, and said, "My baby sister is in here."

The following day, my stepmother visited the doctor because she wasn't feeling well. A pregnancy test confirmed she was positive. My sister ~~censored~~ was born on June 20, 1998.

For later reference, my ability to provide a "psychic ultrasound" became a way to "test" my abilities. I have seven sisters (six sharing the same father) and two brothers (both sharing the same father). All are half-siblings. I am also the oldest. Including the half-siblings of my half-siblings, step-siblings, etc., the number of us jumps to almost 50.

AI Depiction of Psychic Child Sensing His Unborn Sibling

It is worth noting that among my siblings, I am the only one with an extensive history surrounding the supernatural. While others have had experiences, mostly involving potential spirits, none have revealed to me if they, too, had potential extraterrestrial encounters.

April 1999

Location: Aurora, Colorado

My family had decided to take a road trip to Colorado to visit my uncle and his wife. Growing up, my uncles (my mother's brothers) were often like my own older siblings, and this one was the fun one who taught me what I know about computers. During our stay, there was a single day of tense stress... as if something major was happening. I remembered seeing police cars rushing past the apartment complex my uncle lived, and naturally was curious about what was going on. It was then I started to see myself seemingly flying through the air to follow the cars, and hearing loud bangs from inside the large building. I approached closer, but something withdrew me back into my body.

At the age of three I had my first remote viewing experience. It just came so naturally to me, I didn't have to force it. But the incident that sparked this sequence of events was something that no child should have to witness... the Columbine Massacre. I would not comprehend that this was in fact what I witnessed for years... its not as if there's anyone I can really consult in how to process an event I was not technically even present for.

Date: November, 1999 estimated (by court records)

Location: Earth - United States – Idaho

At the age of three, my stepmother attempted to resolve custody disputes between my mother and father by stabbing me in the back of the neck with a ballpoint pen.

My father was possessive, and he, along with others on that side of the family, frequently reported my mother for suspected abuse. All claims were unfounded. My mother's attempts to report my father were largely ignored, at least according to what I was told, though the reliability of this source is questionable. Custody was shared.

One night, while staying at my father's place, he was soon to get off work. My younger sister, ~~censored~~, and I were in the living room watching TV. My stepmother took ~~censored~~, presumably to get her ready for bed. Moments later, I felt a sharp pain in the back of my neck.

AI Depiction of the "Dragon Man"

I briefly saw a vision of a dark void, dimly lit by an orange-red light source. A tall, menacing being with rough gray skin and reptilian eyes appeared. At the time, for my age, me looked like some kind of "dragon man." He knelt down and spoke to me without moving his lips. The color of his skin may have been altered due to the flames. His voice was deep and raspy, almost growling. He claimed the world was corrupt and that people like my father and stepmother shouldn't be allowed to continue hurting others. He offered to help me fight back, even kill them, if I worked with him.

The temptation was strong, but another voice, more human and caring, intervened in a panic. Without hesitation, I knew to trust it as it screamed, "Dakota, don't listen to him. Fight back."

I let out a war cry, somehow materializing a club in my hands, and struck the tall orange being on the head. Surprised and enraged, the being was about to retaliate when I was transported away in a blinding flash. I glimpsed the arms of a tall gray figure with wings made of energy rather than flesh and feathers.

I returned to the locked bedroom. The caring voice whispered, "Stay strong, we are always watching over you."

The next thing I remember, police officers escorted me outside. I tried to explain that I was just defending myself, but they couldn't believe a three-year-old could do such a thing. They ignored everything my mother and I said. It was my grandmother, my mom's mother, who pointed out the pen mark on the back of my neck.

Dates: 2000 - 2003 estimated

Location: Earth - United States – Idaho

There were several nights I would "dream" of being aboard spacecraft, seeing UFOs in the sky, and talking with strange people in weird uniforms of various colors. Many of them were humanoid; though there were others that resembled mantis, Egaroth, and various others.

Date: August, 2000 estimated

Locations: Earth - United States – Idaho

When I was at the age of five, my mother started showing signs of pregnancy. She soon married my stepfather -censored-. I once again predicted this child was a girl who would become my younger sister -censored-. -censored- and my mother would be divorced by September 10, 2001. The marriage only lasted about three months.

Date: September 10th, 2001

My mother's divorce from stepfather. I'm noting this as a "reference event" to help in maintaining accuracy in the timeline. Being that I sucked at keeping records and didn't really acknowledge these events until later in life, the obvious gap makes it so details are obscured.

But the day before the 9/11 attacks on the World Trade Center, my mom's divorce from my stepfather was finalized. We were living with my grandparents after he threw us out, not knowing my mother was pregnant with his daughter at the time.

Date: March 12, 2002

Sister ~~censored~~ was born

Date(s): Summer to possibly early Fall 2002 estimated

Location: Earth - United States - Idaho - Jerome → Spaceships → Murtaugh

One night, at my mother's house in Jerome, Idaho, I went to bed around 6:00 or 6:30 p.m. The exact date is unclear, but the event remains inexplicably strange. When I awoke, it was dark, and my mother had gone to bed. Tall gray beings, known as X5, surrounded me. I wanted to scream for help but couldn't move as one of the beings tossed me over its shoulder. As I was taken out of the room, I saw two more of the grays monitoring my mother, who appeared to be sleepwalking. I tried to call out to her, but no sound escaped. She must have heard my initial screams because the room was illuminated by an ominous blue light, accompanied by an electronic humming. She saw me being taken but, with a wave of the hand from one of the beings, she drifted back to sleep. I remember levitating through the roof, still trying to scream for help.

The craft I was taken aboard appeared silver, but seemed to blend into the night sky, likely a cloaking measure. I watched my house shrink as we ascended. A force rendered me into a mindless state as I was undressed and laid on a table with various instruments being prepared for use. I disassociated, knowing I was in danger but believing no one could save me. I saw holograms of other Greys, more sinister in appearance. I later learned these were Maytra, a race considered hostile parasites by the rest of the galaxy. The Maytra seemed to be communicating orders to the X5, but their transmissions were cut off as something rammed the ship. As the beings started using their tools, the ship was ambushed by a group of three individuals in protective suits.

AI Depiction of Dakota's Abduction

The ship rocked, and the grays screamed in panic. Amid the chaos, I was quickly recovered and taken to my rescuers' ship. A tall blonde woman stayed close to me through the ordeal. Her hair was a golden blonde, her eyes a sparkling blue, and she wore a skin-tight bluish-green uniform. She reminded me of the anime character Sailor Moon, though I wouldn't become familiar with the show until later.

I asked the woman who she was and why she looked familiar. Her voice was soothing, and there was a gentle glimmer in her eyes. With a smile, she told me we had been very good friends for a long time. She seemed to know every question running through my mind without me saying anything. She grabbed my clothes and led me to a table, asking me to lie down so she could check if I was hurt. Despite it being our first meeting, I trusted her completely.

The ship's metals had a blue hue, reflecting the sight outside the front window. A metallic chair rose from the floor, and the woman encouraged me to sit in it. The metal formed to my frame, feeling ticklish. I sat behind two other chairs, all three forming a triangle pattern, allowing me to view Earth through the front window. Instantly mesmerized, I noticed a tall, muscular man with blonde hair in a darkish blue uniform sitting in one of the seats, appearing to be in charge.

I asked the man and woman their names. The man chuckled and smiled. The woman, her eyes sparkling, spoke without moving her lips, "I'm Olivia."

Olivia explained that we had known each other for a long time and were members of a group protecting people from harmful creatures. The reality of the situation hit me: those who took me were aliens. As my heart raced, Olivia hummed a soothing melody. The man explained that none of us were from Earth and that I was part of a project to save people from monsters like the ones who took me. Part of me felt excited, thinking of a group like the X-Men. The two seemed to understand the reference by peering into my mind.

They kindly took me on a joyride in space, showing me close-ups of the Moon, Mars, and Jupiter. After a few hours, the man said it was time to go home. They explained they had to make me forget the encounter to keep me safe. I was upset, not wanting to forget my rescuers or what I saw. Olivia reassured me they would return when I was older and would need my help. She spoke softly, "We are always watching over you," before giving me a hug and asking if I had any other questions.

I asked to be taken to my grandparents' house, feeling safer there. Initially, they hesitated, explaining it wasn't my mother's fault. But I was stubborn, and Olivia convinced the crew to drop me off at my grandparents', assuring I would be returned home.

I remember being carried by Olivia, moving through the unopened window that lead into my bedroom. As she helped me into bed, she placed three fingers against my forehead to help fog my brain, in order to hide the more extravagant details of my adventures from that night. Whether she intentionally gave me a lower dose, did it by accident, or something about my mind helped access parts of these memories; I am not sure. Even with the brain fog, I could remember being taken, the crew that saved me. The biggest thing I remembered was Olivia's eyes.

The next morning, I woke up, unaware of how I got there. My grandparents had no clue I was there. Minutes after I woke up, my mother called, screaming because she couldn't find me. She immediately suspected my dad, an unlikely scenario since I was at her parents' house—thirty miles from where I went to bed.

A map detailing Dakota's abduction, including an estimated location of eyewitnesses

Date: August 19th, 2002

NUFORC Incident Report - Possible Connection

Earth - United States - Idaho - near Twin Falls
UFO Sighting Near Twin Falls - 2002
Date: August 2002
Time: Approximately 11 p.m.
Location: Near Twin Falls, Idaho
Lights on Object: Yes

In August 2002, my husband and I embarked on the first leg of our road trip honeymoon, departing from Seattle in the morning. Around 11 p.m., we decided to find a motel in Twin Falls, Idaho.

As we approached Twin Falls, we saw road signs indicating that the town was only a few miles away. Despite this, we missed the exit and continued driving for a considerable distance before realizing our mistake. We turned around and headed back.

Ahead of us, we initially thought we saw an airplane in the distance, but its flight pattern and speed seemed unusual. As the light approached, we could see the underside of the object, and we both immediately recognized it as a UFO. The lights on the underside were rotating.

The object never came close enough for us to discern its shape. We parked on the side of the road and watched as the object moved across the sky, eventually disappearing behind some mountains. We then resumed our drive toward Twin Falls.

Upon reaching our destination, we confirmed that we had indeed missed Twin Falls and two exit signs. We were not keeping track of the time closely, so we cannot confirm if there was any missing time. However, it remains a mystery how two attentive people could overlook two exit signs.

NOTE: This corresponding report was taken from the NUFORC website, and is not in any way shape or form a claim of ownership. The only changes made were for spelling and grammar purposes. I chose to include this as the timing and location leads me to believe this is connected to a likely abduction I experienced as a child. If by some chance the couple from the report sees this, please reach out if you can.

4

Growing Up and Taking Aim

April, 2004

Earth - United States - Idaho - Murtaugh School → Boise

School field trip to the state capital, Boise. Had an incident at the Old Idaho Penitentiary where I saw an apparition hanging on death row. No one believed me, mostly my fault

Entrance to the Old Idaho State Penitentiary

© Dakota Frandsen

from spending most of my time trying to scare the girls in my class.

As our group was taking a tour of the prison, we went up to the second floor of the execution chamber where the noose was on display. As the group started to leave a man who was tied at the wrists and legs was walking towards the noose. I watched as the rope was secured around his neck, and the floor opened beneath him. Problem was the rope wasn't secured correctly, in order to snap the man's neck. He just hung there, suffocating.

I tried talking about my story, but no one believed me due to reasons mentioned early. However a few years later when the Ghost Adventures came through town for their first season, they captured a shadow apparition on Death Row, identifying the man as Raymond Snowden. Snowden is often referred to as "Idaho's Jack the Ripper," sentenced to prison after violently stabbing a woman who resisted his advances. He claimed to have killed three other women, but this was never proven. Snowden was the man I saw.

Spring, 2004

Earth - United States - Idaho - Murtaugh → Twin Falls

Had to get my tonsils and adenoids removed at the age of nine. For some reason blood samples would either disappear or "pooled after collection," requiring further blood draws to be done. When I would have to be taken to a parent facility in Boise later in life for separate medical incidents, the doctors there questioned why it would be done in the first place.

The Twin Falls hospital does not have the best reputation, the facility covered up a number of lawsuits. Most legal proceedings are handled by the parent facility in Boise due to number of malpractice lawsuits that continue to pile up and be hidden away.

SEVERAL OCCASIONS, 2005-2006:

AI Depiction of a proud child messaging his father who is deployed in the military

My father suddenly tries to make contact, as he was being shipped over to Iraq. Shortly after the attacks on September 11th, my father enlisted in a local National Guard branch in one the very few moments I could have to say I was proud he was my dad, and for a time I was. I was naive, and did want a relationship with my father in spite of earlier incidents. The only hitch was I was still nervous around my stepmother, despite everyone assuming I had completely blocked out the knife incident. How could I when to this day my oblivious mother continues to bring it up in conversations with strangers and specifically worded it to make me sound like a monster? Oh well, I guess...

Conversations between my father and I took place mostly online through early morning instant messaging. As -censored- was old enough to use a computer, the same applied to her. No one ever stopped to realize I was doing all I could to avoid my stepmother. About 6 months after he had returned from deployment, my sister -censored- was born... fully grown.

Visitations with my father became more prevalent, but a hidden darkness seemed to try to grasp my attention. My abilities started to appear, knowing that my life was potentially in danger, making my own skin feel uneasy around both my father and stepmother. I constantly felt I needed to be on high alert, in case I needed to make a run for it.

AI Depiction of young boy noticing signs of abuse

I should've stayed away, but my attention kept returning to them as more siblings were born in the years to follow. My brothers -censored- were born, after my stepmother had an alleged miscarriage. It was also roughly this time period she had started to take pills, later to be pointed out to be acid. As time went on I noticed the abuse seemed to focus on Addison, going as far as my father dragging her into a bedroom and to be followed by a series of screams. My stepmother did nothing to stop it. It was after this I wanted nothing to do with my father unless witnesses were present. Public place, only the kids, or at my grandfather's place were the conditions I wanted... of course no one listened. It should be noted my stepmother would frequently tell my younger siblings to not tell anyone the "family secret," whenever they would go to a large gathering of people. I didn't catch it at the time, or if I did I never got an answer and would soon forget the matter.

December 2005

Earth - United States - Idaho - Murtaugh

More supernatural encounters take place during a dreadful Christmas program I was forced into (I was never really into school activities). Most appearing as strange objects appearing in my grandmother's photos. With most paranormal photos, orbs manifested but these were very unusual. Unlike most orbs which were reflections of water and dust in the air, these had features that would make hardcore skeptics consider the possibility of ghostly happenings. The first was a bright yellow orb, with a distorted face in the middle and lightning filling the "body." The second was a green partial orb with feet! The third was a shadow of one of my friends facing the opposite direction as the rest of the group. Unfortunately these photos were lost in time despite my efforts to try and retrace what happened to them.

SUMMER, 2006:

Earth – United States - Idaho

Father discharged from service, possibly dishonorable. Abuse on ~~censored~~ worsens. I stayed away this time upon getting the indication no more children would emerge via my "sources," though later revelations would indicate my stepmother had more miscarriages. It should be noted that the signs of rather dark activities involving many parties were always quite clear but my somewhat naive mindset at the time wasn't able to process it all, even the mind I carry at the age of 22 (how old I was at the time of this initial addition to this listing) still struggles to comprehend the first hand knowledge of it all.

November 23rd, 2006

Earth - United States - Idaho - Murtaugh → Twin Falls → Boise

Thanksgiving my gall bladder gave out. I was staying with my grandparents while my mom worked. While normally a day I would practically be stalking the kitchen, I mostly slept as I was not feeling well, barely able to eat a bite of ice cream and a turkey sandwich.

AI Depiction of Supernatural Being Coming to Aid

That night I had a sharp pain in my side, violently getting sick from anything my grandmother tried to give me to help. I was rushed to the hospital, where I was deemed to be going into renal failure. The doctors at the hospital said my case was too severe but the parent facility in Boise would be willing to take me.

While on the hospital ride I would cycle in and out of consciousness. I remember seeing flashes of the stereotypical description of "Heaven," with my deceased relatives watching with others as I seemed to flicker in and out. They were confused as to why I was there so soon, only led to asking somewhat panicked questions when they would be seeing me just phase in and out.

Hospital in Boise verified that I was going into renal failure. My gallbladder had shut down, infecting the rest of my system. They managed to get me stabilized but said I would likely need surgery to remove my gallbladder. I was in the hospital for a month to recover.

Throughout the ordeal I remember visitors stopping by, other than relatives. Some were the deceased relatives who crossed over, others were patients in the hospital who were already dead or close to it, others may have been "star family," trying to offer words of encouragement and helping stabilize my system from their side. Apparently the disruption in this physical vessel was reflected in my other body. Possible quantum entanglement. My alter ego / higher self (whatever the heck people call it) seemed to thrash about from inside the pod while alerts were sent of the disturbance.

January 19th, 2007

Earth - United States - Idaho - Twin Falls → Boise

I Depiction of Human and Alien Medical Intervention

Surgery to have my gallbladder removed got moved to my eleventh birthday. I was in the fifth grade. I remember brief dreams of what I now know is a medical ship similar to the Excelsior, an alien mothership tied to the GFW. I looked older than I was, mid-20s. And I had hair. Before the surgery a woman came up and explained that others would be posted at the hospital to keep an eye on my Terran body while it recovered. Once again, blood samples would mysteriously disappear.

There were complications during the surgery, excess swelling in the abdomen that had to be cut away. It seemed that if the surgery hadn't been forced to change dates, I could've been in some serious trouble.

While in recovery, for a couple more weeks, I remember flashes of the stasis pod bay. My consciousness seemed to directly switch between both vessels thanks to the state I was in.

FALL, 2008:

Fights at school, and at home, start to drive my mind into dark places leaving suicide as an option. Around this time, I moved in with my maternal grandparents as well, leaving me to attend school with a group of rather prejudiced individuals I thought were friends. My grandparents lived in the small town of Murtaugh, and I spent some time in my elementary school years growing up there. My childish, naive mindset made me believe these people were my friends. The people there seemed friendly but the second they found out that an individual was not a member of the local church, that individual was treated as an outcast. Just about anyone who left the area could back me up on this statement.

The constant conflict made it so I would start planning how I would end my own life. Upon a warm fall night, I decided it was time. In my bedroom was a large closet with metal railings that looked sturdy enough to hold my weight. I had decided the best method to approach this was to hang myself from the railing using an old belt. The closet itself wasn't very high and I have always been tall for my age, making the attempt somewhat of a challenge. I didn't want anyone to stop me, and I tried to mask any noise I made to make it just seem like I was having a rough night's sleep.

AI Depiction of being a Social Outcast

To counter the challenge, I set a chair in a spot where my feet could touch it just enough to focus my weight more towards my head as I dangled. The plan was to kick the chair back and cut off blood flow. The belt would squeeze tighter till I was deprived of oxygen… maybe that was what triggered it.

I honestly cannot say if my plan had worked, or if the "intervention," had timed its arrival to stop me; but the following spooked me nonetheless. In what would've been my final moments, something caused my body to freeze. A bright blue light emerged out of nowhere, completely overriding my senses. The energy from it was so intense, it made my surroundings vanish; giving the appearance I was floating. I took a few moments to look around, as my eyes were the only parts of my body that could move and saw light dance as if I was deep underwater.

AI Depiction of Mysterious Figure

Suddenly a man appeared before me; his image blurred. I could tell he had long brown hair and facial hair, and wore what looked like a white robe. The vibe I was receiving from his presence felt calm, friendly, and concerned about my well being. My external senses tried to give me an indication someone else was nearby, but my focus was centered on what was unfolding before me to really take notice. The man walked closer to me, his image looking clearer as he approached. Soon he starts to speak. No judgment, no criticism, just concern.

"Dakota, there is someone here that you should meet."

The man stepped aside and revealed a young girl, roughly the age of five or six. She had long blonde hair, somewhat tan skin, and the brightest blue eyes I'd ever seen. Immediately, I could tell the little girl was kin to me as she had a striking resemblance to my sisters. Tears filled her eyes making them sparkle like the ocean on a blissful summer day, instantly sending my heart into a deep abyss as the sensation of guilt overcame me.

But it wasn't her appearance that pulled me out of that trance, rather it was what she said to me. She approached me, placed her hand on my cheek, and cried, "Daddy, please don't do it."

As the little girl leaned in to kiss me on the cheek the vision disappeared and I am back in the closet like nothing happened. I tried to

AI Recreation of "Olivia"

created by Dakota Frandsen, 2021

shake off what I had seen by going to bed but the image would find ways to interfere in future events. Her interference lead to me giving her the name "Olivia Hope," after the name was passed on to me through "future" experiments meant to help me try to make contact with her to understand what I had witnessed.

SPRING, 2009:

After a few chats with a love interest and a "coming to Jesus" meeting with one of my uncles I had decided to move back in with my mother as Murtaugh was not the place for me. It held answers as to what I needed to do in order to progress. My thoughts centered on finding Olivia's mother, but in order to do so I needed to try to get answers from my little girl. I knew the possibility of time paradoxes of these attempts, and just how likely it was my daughter would know it was well; I had to try. Research on various online forums and radio podcasts revealed several possible methods I could try to make contact; as my previous experiences proved the possibility of latent psychic powers.

The method that seemed easiest to work with was automatic writing. For the uninitiated, automatic writing is a form of spiritual channeling that allows for the "spirit" to take over control of the hands belonging to the "channeler" and would allow for them to convey messages in writing. I must note that such a process can easily be hijacked by negative beings, doing such experiments can be highly dangerous, but I was desperate enough for answers.

Naturally, my first target was my seemingly time traveling daughter. Experiments with making contact seemed to be successful, for the most part. Each session I was able to establish it was her and got her to answer a few questions. The question set for the sessions went something along these lines (as it was recovered from an old notebook I dug up):

I am looking to make contact with the little girl who saved me...

Is this little girl who referred to me as "Daddy?"

Spirit: "Yes"

Are you actually my daughter?

Spirit: "Yeah"

About when will you be be here?

Spirit: "2025" (*time travel? This was before aliens were contemplated... then again 2024 is supposed to be about when the human looking ETs reveal themselves. Different sessions alternated between the years 2024 and 2025)

What is your name?
Spirit: "Olivia"
What is your favorite color?
Spirit: "Green"

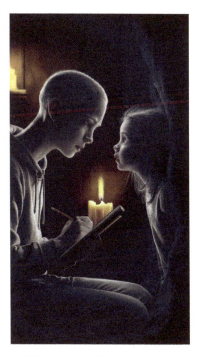

AI Depiction of Dakota's attempt to contact Olivia

Do you have any siblings?
Spirit: "Yes. A brother, Michael."

I tried to format the questions to get a general idea of my daughter's personality, as well as what the future may have had in store for me. When I finally worked up the courage to ask for Olivia's mother's name, one of two things would happen. Either my head would fill with what sounded like radio interference and I would lose the connection to her, or Olivia would say she wasn't able to reveal that much at the moment.

But, if I didn't make it clear before, this was not going to be our last encounter.

LATE FALL, 2010:

Further research on paranormal activity leads to my decision to pursue paranormal investigations but being I was barely in high school, I had no funding source other than occasional babysitting payments my family would brush up on me whenever I grew frustrated by constantly having to watch my younger relatives.

Paranormal investigation was an expensive hobby, especially at the extent I wanted to take it, so I was forced to wait out for holiday and birthday gifts when babysitting wasn't as fruitful. I started reaching out, through social media, to others in the field to start studying and getting ideas on how to put together my own team. I was forming the Paranromal Raider Force, something to stick out from the so called "serious investigators."

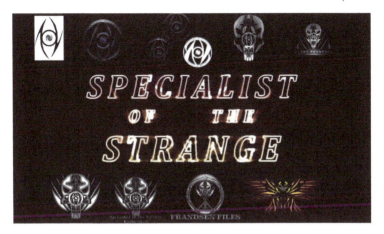

Various logos designed by Dakota Frandsen

circa. 2011 - 2020

Further notes came from watching the various paranormal shows on television. My main idea was to watch the shows to get ideas for tech and methods, then tinker until I had a fitting practice. It would work rather quickly in my favor, as I used the fact most assumed my age to be almost double what it actually was to my advantage. A local radio DJ outed me, but by then most were impressed enough by what I had built on my own that my age was not a concern.

This was comforting in many aspects, as one of the things that motivated my decision to pursue this life, and maybe build a name for myself around it, was the fact that this was about when my father was imprisoned for sexually assaulting my sister -censored-. Being that I was around them, I was mostly kept away from the investigation. However this didn't settle knowing that my siblings from him were being placed into foster care. My youngest sister at the time, ~~censored~~ who I had yet to meet, was only six months old. My mentality was dirtied enough that the Hatman, as he's dubbed, made an appearance offering to take care of my father for me. Part of it felt like he understood the turmoil in me, but I promptly told him to fuck off. This would not be the last of him.

APRIL, 2010:

I met my high school sweetheart.

Springtime, halfway through my freshman year, I had met a beautiful girl in class. The class was Touchstones, it was supposed to "help" kids figure out how to move on to the important milestones we were supposed to reach in our teen to young adult life. Early on in the class, I noticed this shy red head that usually kept to herself. Her name was ~~censored~~. I had tried to think of a way to conveniently bump into ~~censored~~ (I gave her the

AI Depiction of Dakota meeting "Shandra"

name of Shandra in my *The Ones Who Walk All Worlds* series) so I was able to ignite the flame, but could never patch one together until the teacher of that class assigned us both to the same group for a skit. The skit was supposed to resemble scenarios out of a self described "teen self help" book meant to teach better ways to react to stressful situations any average Joe could run into on a day to day basis. My group was given a skit meant to depict some jackass cutting off someone in traffic, resulting in a wreck.

The group was comprised of ~~censored~~, myself, and a few classroom idiots. ~~censored~~ being shy, stayed separated from the group. As the idiots discussed the skit, I made a point to introduce myself to her to light the flame. She tried to shy away but I was able to get her to open up. Read the first entries of *The Ones Who Walk All Worlds,* if you want an idea how that conversation turned out.

Soon, she would become the first "patient" I would lose. We got into an altercation when a third member of our group joined, turning the situation into a love triangle. I didn't handle the situation well, she was getting close to someone who was becoming physical abusive towards women and the very thought churned my stomach.

April 23rd 2011

Earth - United States – Idaho - Murtaugh

Noted: The first ever investigation as the Paranormal Raider Force took place in the Highway Department Building.

Paranormal Raider Force Logo
circa 2014

The initial plan was to look into strange noises that suggested a residual type haunt. Two faces, an old lady screaming, footsteps, and flaring motion sensors later we learn that these spirits are very willing to make themselves known. A side case at the time was looking for a toddler that had been seen around some nearby train track wielding a chainsaw which was believed to show itself, in photos, as a green orb with feet. Not much time was invested in this phenomena due to the approaching coyotes and the fact right next to the area in which the sighting occurred is a bar.

I had finally gathered enough decent equipment to actually hold a well orchestrated investigation. An offer from my grandfather to check out his place of work came at a convenient time, since I was staying at my grandparents for the weekend while my mother recovered from surgery.

The location was Murtaugh Highway Department, believed to be haunted by former employees and the old foreman of the location. Reports came in to strange smoke, the shop doors rattling without wind or passing semi trucks, footsteps, and occasional disembodied voices. One of the alleged spirits was my grandfather's old boss, who apparently had kids that went to school with my parents; his cause of death was lung cancer... same for his wife. Both were heavy smokers in their lifetime.

Due to my age at the time, the state of Idaho has a curfew law for anyone under 16, I was accompanied by my grandmother. I was 15 by the time I landed this investigation. I was originally against the idea, noting my grandmother's tendency to try to control a situation, and my desire to keep any and all activities outside of my family's control (which they would do on a few occasions). But in this situation having my grandmother on board would prove useful.

Screenshot of Mysterious Face

I published the results of the investigation, with brief case reports, as a YouTube video to help promote business. The case was able to gather strange faces making appearance on a video camera and strange audio recordings. Off camera, was a screaming woman's voices during setup, footsteps moving through the gravel, and voices coming through a radio session.

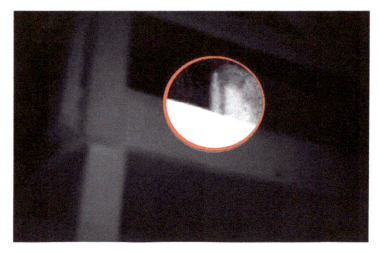

A Second Figure Captured on a Stairwell

The radio session was an idea to try and replicate results from the infamous Ghost Boxes without any tinkering. The idea was to simply set an available radio to the lowest possible frequency to make it easier for spirits to communicate. The snag was making sure nothing was coming through on the selected frequency. This location has been the only spot it seemed to work.

Through this and a follow up (mentioned below), I have deemed "Murtaugh Highway Department" as a legitimate haunting site.

SPRINGBREAK, 2011:

Earth → United States → Idaho → Twin Falls

During spring break of my freshman year in high school, I was involved in a car accident during my driver's ed class. I was the driver of the vehicle, but was not found at fault. The drive was scheduled to take those of us in my group at the time out into the county and on the freeway. As we came back into town, an old lady tried to dart through six lanes of busy traffic. Obviously, as should be indicated by the inclusion of this event, I was the one to strike her. The old lady tried to plead innocence and reason with the officer but she was the one found at fault in what the cop himself described was much like a failed game of "Frogger." On impact it felt like I was thrown into an astral project, seeing the car crush on the front end as I was rendered unconscious.

JULY 2-4th, 2011:

Earth → United States → Idaho → Sawtooth National Forest → Near Diamondfield Jack

My first Sasquatch investigation.

AI Depiction - Promotional Thumbnail for FrandsenFiles: South Hills Sasquatch

As my grandfather continued his battle with cancer, the family decided to take everyone camping rather than doing our usual drive to Wyoming for illegal fireworks then lighting them off for the Fourth of July. One of the locations that was being considered was of interest as it was the area I spotted a possible Sasquatch years earlier. There is a series of caves near the Magic Mountain ski resort a family of 'Squatch seem to reside in. Given the timeframe of the appearances, and the possible age of the juvenile I was able to encounter, at least four specimens are in the region.

I received a possible tip earlier that week about Sasquatch dietary preferences to help lure one out from a news video that was circulating depicting a retired forensics analyst utilizing pieces of chocolate to lure a specimen in front of a trail camera. A small ape-like creature approached me from behind as I was setting things up, but quickly bolted when it realized I knew it was there. Its fur was almost black, it was dark out, and the little monster was fast.

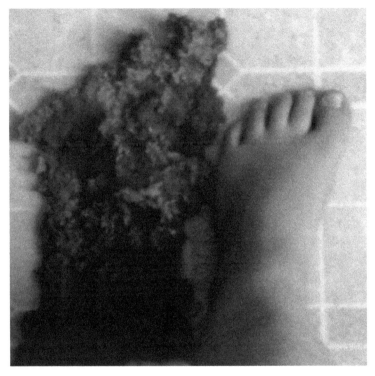

"Bigfoot" Casting Comparison to US Man's Sized 18 Foot

I didn't have a trail camera at my disposal for this hunt, but I did have soft enough ground to gather a foot casting should I be successful. The second night into the trip, I finally laid the trap but had fallen asleep before any appearance was made. The following morning I was able to examine the area and successfully extract a foot casting. My estimates show the possible specimen had a foot large enough to fit a man's size 22 shoe… my own foot being a size 18. Unfortunately years later the casting was destroyed while moving to a new residence, but I have this photo comparison to show that I did not fake the casting since I was the person with the largest stature and foot size. Comparisons I made with photos from a University of Idaho professor who hunts Bigfoot himself show striking resemblance.

I should also note during the entire stay at the campsite, signs of some sort of a larger animal stalking the area were prevalent but no one was able to confirm exactly what.

Conveniently I was able to catch a radio interview with a show titled "Second Sight," that had a guest star who was a renowned Bigfoot hunter and was able to gather notes of what to look for to possibly track a Sasquatch, which paired with the news segment I mentioned earlier in this listing, provided valuable insight. A few weeks later I was able to contact the same guest on the show and was able to relay my story, landing me a guest appearance on his own show called "Monster Theater."

5

Becoming the Man

AUGUST 13, 2011:

AI Depiction of Angered Spirit

My grandfather had informed me of an incident at his work, which sparked interest and a slight fit of rage with the conditions present at this time. My grandfather, who was near bone thin due to cancer treatments, and my uncle were possibly attacked by a spirit. The incident as reported to me, was that while sitting in the main office, a shelf was ripped from the wall and thrown towards them. Based on the report, the attack seemed to be aimed towards my uncle; knowing how he could've easily mocked the idea of the spirits in general thinking no one would hear him I must acknowledge the possibility he may have had the attack coming. But, that did not excuse attacking a man who was dying!

I did the investigation, with the sole purpose of angering the spirits in the building, and letting them know the attack was not going to be tolerated. I had researched methods to potentially drive out spirits from the location, and had threatened to utilize them if such an incident happened again. Either because of my stature, or that they knew I was serious, there was almost non-existent activity.

Throughout the night I felt as if I was being watched, but could never get the "watchers" to screw up and reveal themselves. As the night went on, a new idea came to mind that I thought could potentially help get some sort of reaction from the residing spirits. What if they just wanted to be left alone?

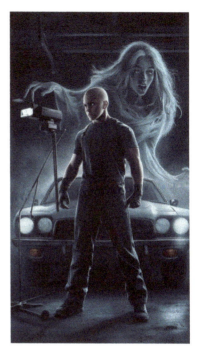

AI Depiction of Dakota on a Ghost Hunt

Using a motion sensor as the trigger object, I offered up the following terms... no more attacks, no more visits from me. They could stay, hell if they felt like pulling pranks on the living that was fine, but no more attacks. If I had made any further appearances, they were to be taken as me simply passing through since my grandfather was still working there and visitations on my part was likely.

Up until the date of August 22, 2017 no further reports of paranormal activity at this location have reached my files. This renders the location to be classified as no longer haunted.

FALL, 2011:

~~censored~~ Announcement

A program to set up to establish the first human colony on Mars by the year 2035 and I was contacted to potentially join the first launch. While the program is an interesting prospect and it could pave the way for entirely new face of humanity, two problems are faced with the idea of me being a part of the launch... 1. I'm five inches too tall and 2. I was younger then the main players for this company thought I was. However the chance to be a part of a historic event such as colonization of another planet is too good an offer to pass up, so I decided to at least put my name in the hat just to see what would happen. A part of me was trying to mentally alleviate the stress I was putting myself under by comparing the name of the company to the DOOM video game, stating a

AI Depiction of Dakota Contemplating a Martian Future

company under a similar name was among the first expeditions to initiate a literal Hell invasion.

The irony behind that statement...

OCTOBER 31, 2011:

I had the chance to go hiking with one of my uncles and my grandparents just past Sun Valley, while they went hunting. The only two reasons I bothered to go, since I'm just not into traditional hunting, was because I was told abandoned mine shafts were in the area and I like to check out wildlife. High amounts of quartz were also in the area, which is a mineral believed to act like a battery source for spirits.

AI Depiction of Dakota Climbing a Steep Mountain

Once we came across the mine shafts in question it felt someone was on the inside looking right back at us and a couple photos seemed to reinforce the notion.

I took home a large quartz chunk, managed to save the photos and show them off to a few individuals that had been on ghost hunting shows... their opinions suggested they felt it was a good capture.

But the biggest lesson I had in this? Do not push yourself past the point of physical exhaustion just to outdo your loud-mouth cousin... your body will make you regret it.

DECEMBER 4, 2011:

Perhaps the most heartbreaking moment of my life in my earliest years on the job, the day I lost the one family member that actually felt the most supportive of my endeavors. It should be obvious by now that my grandfather was more of a dad to me than my own father, and he extended that courtesy to my sister and cousins on my maternal side. But because I was the oldest of the bunch, I had the closest relationship with him. While we all had taken a loss the day he died, it hit me the hardest; though my seemingly lack of emotion caused concern for the rest of the family.

My grandfather was the type of guy who didn't want to be made a big fuss over, and my grandma and I were the only two who remembered this. While everyone continued to fight and prod over how to handle family affairs, she and I were the ones who wanted to simply get past everything and move on. My own mother tried to pry me into bursting down into tears, going as far as saying I wasn't human, on several occasions which continued to build the urge to smash a glass bottle and jam the shards deep into her temple. I didn't trust her with showing any emotion because it would be turned against me, or be used to talk about me like I was nothing more than a mindless ape when I was in the room; hell I still don't trust her in my 20s and our relationship had improved.

But back to my grandpa, though I still miss him, I have to admire how long he managed to hold up against his cancer despite it continually spreading throughout his body. For the service, my grandmother had him cremated and his urn was placed on a display table between two large monitors (this taking place at a funeral home) as a video showing a series of photos from my grandfather's life played. Seeing him as a kid, to old photos of my grandparents together, to the most recent of me and my cousins... this all made me start to reflect on the type of person I wanted to be in this life.

Dakota Aged 4 with his Grandfather - Filters Applied for Privacy

I've always known that I wanted to be just like my grandfather, but it wasn't until after his death I was starting to piece together what all that really meant. Those thoughts continued through dinner that night, as we spent the night in Jackpot to dine out at a casino my grandmother used to work for, and really those thoughts still linger with me today.

Which leads me to this point I want to make for any younger readers seeing this, particularly the young adults in the stage of life where they believe they won't need their parents when they turn 18.

Though my grandpa wasn't my biological parent, he was more of a parental figure then my own mother and father and as I am now 28 at the time of writing this entry, I can tell you in full honesty that I wish I still had him with me today to sort out life. When I know it's time to move up in the world, how to make a good impression, all of the typical father-son moments, how to be a good dad when my own kids come along, to knowing when he knew my grandmother was the one... I find myself asking him these things only to be met with an echo of his voice that still resides inside my head.

On some occasions the voices provide clues, but nevertheless I am still met with silence and the annoyances of having to piece together all of those on my own. Hell, I wish at times I wasn't such a brat when he tried to teach me about cars. But needless to say, I wish he was still here because I've come to accept the fact there is much more to the world I have to learn. So if you can, don't be quick to toss out your parents, or whoever steps up to properly fill that role in your life.

LATE DECEMBER, 2011:

My emotions from having just lost my grandfather became tested as I learned of someone I thought of as a friend struck a young lady in our class. To go from the best of my memory, ~~censored~~ struck this young lady after she called him out for his behavior towards women. I do not care for jackasses that do that to girls no matter the situation. I tried to avoid him, knowing I was going to do something careless out of anger but I could not avoid letting my face reveal my true intentions. -censored- did try to confront me, which is where I let him have it. I even promised to kill him if he tried to put his hands on another girl ever again. My message got through to him, as he was soon escorted around school by teachers and eventually moved to Arizona with relatives. He was out of sight, that's all I cared about.

As for me, I was put into what was called "PASS (Positive Alternative to School Suspension) Room" for the one class -censored- and I shared, just to help ease tensions. Though the next day, when I showed up to the designated room, the main teacher informed me that the notice never actually went through. I stayed just to avoid further issues. -censored- saw me as I left, which apparently moved her to ask around about what happened and our final blowout which lead to the breakup of the "team" took place.

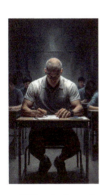

AI Depiction of Dakota in P.A.S.S. Room

It's not like we were gonna last anyways.

Truth be told, this only lead me to dive further into the supernatural as a way to keep myself in check. One of the subjects I'd start researching more of is demonology, even looking into how to summon a demon if I were to ever end up in a truly desperate enough situation. I scoured through the lore and found one that caught my eye the most, a being named Marchosias.

Some say Marchosias can appear as male, some say female, other who saw the demonic form saw a wolf with wings and a snake for a tail. What attracted me the most to this particular being was that Marchosias, according to the "lore" wasn't necessarily fond of the idea of the angels falling, in fact hoping that differences can be mended and both sides can return to Heaven. Her choice to fall was because she had family also fell.

When I conducted the ritual, the summoning was a bit more successful than I anticipated

JANUARY 7, 2012:

Rumors of a possible spirit haunting the halls of a local elementary school lingered as my mother held a position at the playground for work. Initially I tried to schedule the investigation close to when my mother first started working there but her nerves about approaching the boss too quickly led to me having to hold back until this date. The principal was a family friend and she happened to attend my grandfather's funeral, so seeing people she would trust under those circumstances helped open up the doors. The only major issue was that ~~censored~~ had to come along due to needing my mother's keys and having no backup babysitter. I was against the idea at first, but figured at the very least having a kid around may stir up some activity.

AI Depiction of Former Principal's Spirit Watching Over Children

The building itself was recently celebrating its 100 year anniversary, and I was informed by the principal that the interior itself was renovated several occasion in that time frame. The investigation, however, proved to be rather dull as all claims were disproved. Chatter in the basement was the rapid clicking of a water heater being twisted by a half tired mind, self flushing toilets were lack of water pressure, and reports of hearing children at play were due to nearby families taking their kids to play on the grounds in the middle of the night. There were parts of the school I didn't have access to in order to disprove any claims, but all in all the location was not haunted.

Students at the school quickly spread rumors, but hopefully they stay just that. Research has shown it may be possible something may emerge if the kids believed in the rumors, causing a manifestation.

JANUARY 27, 2012:

During my grandfather's funeral I was able to land another case. The client was my grandmother's best friend from high school who had mentioned her home was a possible paranormal activity, after my own ventures were brought up in conversation. It seemed the location was plagued by shadow people, voices in the night, and phantom feelings of being touched. It was also brought to my attention that several violent deaths were tied to that location including one decapitated woman.

At least four violent deaths occurred on the premises, the decapitated woman found in a ditch just outside the house. My interest in the location peaked to say the very least.

The house itself looked like an oversize shack that could've easily toppled over with a good enough windstorm, and it was surrounded by much farmland. Old wells were scattered on the premises, a long ditch ran for about a quarter of a mile from the residence... the entire place felt like the setting for a horror show to go down. It quickly proved to be one of the scariest cases I faced.

AI Depiction of Dakota Seeing the Mysterious Well

The ditch outside, right where the body was found, started to glow by itself. This was enough to scare my skeptical uncle who decided to tag along for this case. Voices kept trying to speak up but barely audible enough to hear with the naked ear, cold spots, and phantom "touching" sensations were only the beginning. Evidence review cleared up some of the communications with the other side but one EVP recording soon took the case to new heights; as it was a woman's voice saying she was inside the well.

On the property, in the basement directly below where the tape recording was captured, was a sealed off well. It had a metal plate with some kind of sun symbol on it, partially covered in cement.

What in the hell was in there? I have little clue. But the thing is standing over that thing... just felt like something evil was trying to drag you in.

Evidence collected from this location is perhaps one of the strangest yet. Orbs reflecting off of metal surfaces, the voices, the strange lights... what the hell was going on?

Further investigation was obviously warranted... if the client could've just stayed out of prison.

One last question still lingers about... what the hell was my grandmother into to attract this kind of stuff?

MAY 2012:

I was informed by a mutual friend that -censored- had gone missing, apparently leaving a note behind on Mother's Day of all days to tell her mother she had gone to live with her "street family." Eventually the student resource officer approached me, knowing that there was a point up until recently that -censored- and I seemed rather close and, while he knew I had nothing to do with her disappearance, he asked if by any chance I had heard something. Obviously I didn't, having not spoke to her after the team broke up. but as he and I spoke I noticed that another friend of -censored- was watching intently, a look of panic coming over her. I knew right away she knew something, and would probably be the one link directly to -censored- to figure out where she went.

I utilized this connection to slowly feed information to -censored- in order to trick her into thinking I was closing in her location, to either trick her into coming back or revealing where she was. Being new into the supernatural, I used my early knowledge of police investigation procedure of knowledge to slowly tighten the noose over the next couple weeks. Pairing divination methods my great-grandmother recommended, reported sightings, and simple deduction I managed to get a good idea of where -censored- ended up.

She had left the state with some guy and headed south into Utah. I tried my best to use what I knew of remote viewing to get a rough idea of where she might've been staying, building description and all. When I'd felt confident in my findings, I would ensure that the friend would

AI Depiction of Dakota lost in focus at his ex-girlfriend's missing poster

overhear that I was closing in. After two weeks of searching, it was within 24 hours of me announcing the city -censored- was in that -censored- would eventually call her mother to come get her.

A part of me wanted to see if we could rekindle the old flame, but seeing how every had unfolded it seemed she had some stuff of her own to work through before committing to anything big. I missed her, and the thought of her disappearance worried me greatly. It felt weird seeing her picture on a missing poster hanging on the wall of a local department store. But, at least she was brought home safe.

JUNE 23, 2012:

I found a website that hosts audio broadcasts for free, and contemplation began to start up my own radio show to help keep up appearances and boost my audience. For a while I ran with the title, "Journals of Supernatural Adventure," and the basic premise was I would discuss ideas and theories on various phenomena. The show managed to stay afloat and old recordings still float around on my old Youtube pages of nearly all the episodes I recorded.

JULY 6, 2012:

First episode of Journals of Supernatural Adventure airs. Obviously not many people listened in given the show's new status and lack of funds to pay for marketing.

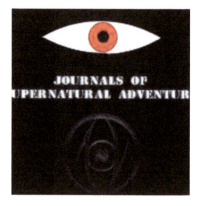

Old Podcast Thumbnail

FALL, 2012:

During my first two years of high school, I went to school at -censored-. Honestly, I hated my time there and during class registration periods nearly all the courses I would choose would get removed from the curriculum. I honestly got tired of this happening because I had a rough idea of what I was wanting to accomplish in life and what little they had to offer me in those regards kept getting pulled so I knew if I were to actually have a chance to do what I wanted to do in life I would have to leave. It was probably one of the best decisions in my life to trick my mother into signing me into -censored- to finish out high school. Had I not done that... a lot of what follows in the next entries probably wouldn't have come together. Yes it was an online school, but at least I would be taking lessons in subjects that actually interested me.

OCTOBER 10, 2012:

Phase 1 of Scrapped Documentary on the Supernatural. Given the extensive nature of what I had yet to learn, it seemed better to just put this project on the shelf until more resources could be allocated for it.

OCTOBER 27, 2012:

JSA Emergency Broadcast for -censored- case. Protection prayer asked of the audience for a family in turmoil. It was quickly proved the source of activity was a pissed off dead mother-in-law who was not too happy with the unfaithful and abusive husband. -censored- soon filed for divorce after I told her what to look for, basing my warnings on the actions of my own father when we started seeing my stepmother while still technically with my mother. Basically, he tried to write off my stepmother as a babysitter for me.

Nevertheless, as much as I almost crossed professional boundaries... this case was a win.

SEPTEMBER 23, 2013:

UFO Fireball Investigation

AI Depiction of Dakota encountering MIB

Green ball of light seen in the sky, causes some property damage to homes in the area where the "light" disappeared. No media coverage, in spite of reports of an explosion and aforementioned property damage. Quickly ruled out as a meteor, rich in iron causing the green flames. Though likely unrelated, I personally saw possible Men in Black within the same week. Three of them, sitting in black SUV, pulled up on a nearby street and just stared at me. No feeling of danger, more of a "you wanted to see us, now what?" sort of vibe. I had been looking into alleged sightings, out my own curiosity, but was not expected to have an actual encounter.

FALL, 2014:

F

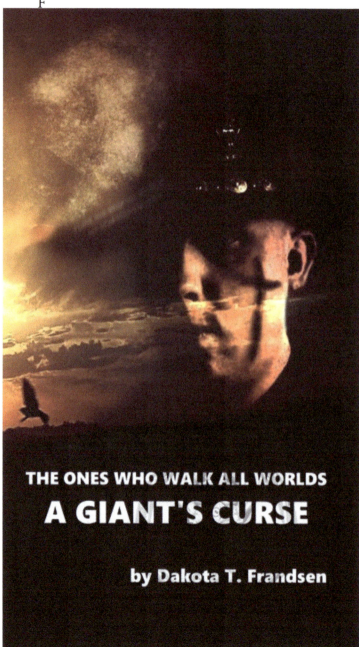

The Ones Who Walk All Worlds: A Giant's Curse Cover

Walk All Worlds," a book series based loosely on my paranormal exploits and understandings of the phenomenon at the time. The book itself has undergone a couple different rereleases, the latest being a collection of all books released under the series as one title, "The Ones Who Walk All Worlds: Origins."

MAY, 2014:

I graduated high school and jumped straight into the workforce rather than attend my graduation or any senior trips. It just felt weird being that I hardly ever actually saw other kids who were in my class, except when we had to go to a local hotel conference room to do our SATs. My mother tried reaching out to my councellor under the assumption I didn't want to do due to her chaotic work schedule, but it honestly couldn't be farther from the truth.

6
Officially an Adult

MAY - AUGUST, 2014:

First job out of school at a local call center. It was an outsourcing company, and because of my knowledge of computers I was assigned to an internet service company that didn't even offer service in my area. What was even more messed up was that any motivation to potentially move up in the company was quickly burnt out when it was revealed the position I was given was the highest one. Moving up to a supervisor, even in the same "area" would require a pay cut.

AI Depiction of Dakota at a Call Center Job

It's not like I wanted to move up, but seriously made me question the motivations of those who tried. Especially when a guy who was in my training group started sleeping with my direct supervisor. Oh well, not like it mattered in the long run anyway. The main reason I applied for the job was because I knew that I would recognize some people who already worked there; my stepmother and my first girlfriend from middle school. My stepmother seemed like she was trying to get her life in order after dealing with my father. As for my ex... enough time had passed and we were both adults now. I also knew from back then she was diagnosed with dissociative identity disorder, or more popularly known as multiple personality disorder.

When I got onto the job, even more familiar faces happened to be hired on at the same time, which did help ease my nerves a bit. Yet in the long run my anxiety got the better of me and I wold start hanging up on customers, leading me to get fired.

OCTOBER, 2014:

I got into a car accident while moving to new house. My grandmother happened to be near the scene and was present as the paramedics helped me get out of the car. Something caused the car, a 2002 Chrysler 300 my grandmother sold me, to start "bucking" randomly while accelerating, giving the impression someone was quickly slamming on the brakes repetitively. As I was helping move a few last minute small items from the old "house" to the new one, this "bucking" started while I was trying to cross an intersection leading me to be struck on the driver's side by a pickup going 60mph. Just moments before impact, Olivia manifested, screaming "Daddy, look out!"

It was too late. I decided to go with the paramedics just to make sure there was no major damage. I was feeling out of it from part of the car frame being slammed into me, had the other driver been going any faster I would've come close to losing my left foot for how far the wheel-well was bent back. Thankfully, in this state and too full of adrenaline, I didn't feel anything and walked myself to the ambulance. During the ride to the hospital I explained to the medics that the reason why I went with them was because after impact, I blacked out and started seeing my deceased grandfather at the end of a tunnel of blue light. CAT scans at the hospital determined no visible brain damage was detected, even though I had dizzy spells for a couple months afterwards.

AI Depiction of the Accident

Because of my mother's connections with local law enforcement, the crash had to be taken by a border jurisdiction. The dispatching facility my mother worked for at the time managed four counties worth of police, fire, and EMS services; the crash took place right on the border of her jurisdiction and another (the exact mapping of what districts were and weren't connected to her can be a bit confusing). However, because of how long my mother had worked the job she still knew quite a few who worked in jurisdictions outside her own.

It was because of this I learned that the officer who took my case wrote the fine on one ticket, that wouldn't be a quick "fix-it" ticket as he called it, at the lowest amount he could get away with. The remaining tickets were easy to get off my record, as they were standard lack of license and registration ones given on account that no one could spot where my wallet landed in the car after it fell out of the loose shorts I was wearing.

I had argued with my mother and grandmother about the fact I had my information on me, rarely ever leaving the house without it. How they would push the issue, emphasizing that how others couldn't find my wallet must somehow magically mean that I was hallucinating having my own wallet on me at the time of impact. It wouldn't be until I had the chance to see the car, a couple days later, at the junkyard so I could recover anything salvageable in it. Even as I started looking, my mother tried insinuating I was trying to make a bigger scene than I was to escape having to pay tickets, only coming to silence when I held my wallet in front of her as even I was starting to doubt myself.

Thankfully a commission payment I had from my previous job came through and that helped me pay off the remaining ticket. I was able to get the ones about not having a license or insurance sorted, as they were the aforementioned "fix-it" tickets.

NOVEMBER 14, 2014:

My mother asked me about a girl I went to school with, after she came home from work. Her job as a ~~censored~~ this was immediately a bad sign. A friend of mine and her mother were gunned down by her stepdad. Unreleased to the media, the stepdad later texted his aunt to confess to his crimes before turning the gun on himself. This information and more was leaked to me, justifying that after a GoFundMe was posted by the family allowed more liberty to discuss the case. And quite frankly, this one hit hard, knowing what I know. I'm not at liberty to discuss the full details, but plenty of people involved carry regret for not doing more.

AI Depiction of Spectral Visit

I was out of a job, didn't have any money on me, but did have a small following thanks to my reputation as the "local teenage ghost hunter."

As I did what I could to help raise money, my friend paid me an ethereal visit through dreamstate to thank me, also revealing everything that happened to her. I had heard through my sources the reason the stepfather did what he did was because my friend's mother discovered he had been sexually assaulting her and she filed for divorce to get the kids away from him. She also admitted to having a crush on me back in school before disappearing. Whether or not this was just a dream, my mind's way of providing closure knowing that it would be impossible for me to have done anything more to help her... I honestly can't say.

I did try for an EVP session afterwards, just once to see if I could confirm the vision of her I saw was just a dream. The audio was weak and required extensive post work to bring out the recording, but it seemed a voice was present confirming my suspicions. Exactly, who was it though?

MARCH 22 - 30, 2015:

Dakota at Tiananmen Square

Towards the end of high school I was nominated to go on a big trip to China. It would've been for the year after I had already graduated but this was an opportunity to fulfill a bit of a bucket list item. The trip was overall amazing, people were friendly, I got treated like the Laughing Buddha. I'm vaguely sure I had some visitations while this took place, the most prevalent was when my group succumbed to likely food poisoning and ended up being hospitalized while in Xi'An about half way through the trip. The only food and drink in our systems was the breakfast from the hotel that morning.

The fact we were just barely flying into Xi'An when we started falling violently ill didn't help at all.

Great Wall of China circa 2015

© Dakota Frandsen

Conditions in the hospital were horrific; understaffed and unclean. Walking into it felt like I was being led to a butcher shop. I was in and out of consciousness from lack of fluids in my system, being yelled at in Mandarin when the IV line would fall out. It seemed like someone in my head was trying to translate but that could've just been my head being twisted. I remember a "displacement" in space and just "floating" through it to a futuristic looking flight deck. I remember a tall blonde man standing next to a woman who was operating a series of holographic panels. There was a brief mention of the word "triad."

I was in and out of consciousness. There was blood drawn to examine for parasitic exposure but all tests allegedly done were inconclusive. However, a male subject was confronted for recording us on camera. Whatever happened to that I do not know.

Temple of Heaven Park, China

© Dakota Frandsen

My paternal grandmother, who had abduction experiences with Grey and alleged hybridized children and claims she can see "angels," made reference to this incident being an attack from the Chinese mafia (as she worded it). I remember brief visions of what looked like the deck of a starship but not much else from it.

SPRING 2014 - WINTER 2015:

It truly pains me that I had such a hard time appropriately documenting this timeframe... as much as it changed my perspective on life. As I am writing this, to finally acknowledge the truth, I came to realize through the help of my therapist that my own perception of the timeline was altered from the trauma. The nightmares just compiled on to what I already fought to suppress, I wish I could've done more for her.

A Memorial Photo of Dakota and his Fiance

Just before I left for China, I joined up on an anonymous messaging board meant for PTSD support groups. Through there, I met a woman, she had initally messaged me asking about something I posted... wanting to know more about feelings I expressed... wanting to fix the world. As time went on we became close, and we officially started dating. The main issue was the distance being across country, and that she literally had discovered she was pregnant. The distance wasn't too much of an issue for me, the China trip gave me the travel bug and I was eager to look for any excuse to get out on the road yet again. The pregnancy should've been a red flag, there was no way I was ready to be a stepfather... and it would be obvious I'd be stepping into a rather complicated situation.

A couple months into the relationship, she decided to get a flight across country to come see me. I was absolutely ecstatic to see her in person but didn't tell many people due to the... baggage. She wanted me to keep it secret as she was trying to escape her abusive ex in order to protect her baby. Much to both our surprises, the baby seemed rather excited to meet me as she would seem more active when her mother and I were speaking.

AI Depiction of the Proposal

During her visit, I did something a bit extreme to show her that I was serious about being there for her. After all she shared with me, it's understandable how she'd be anxious to try settling with a guy. Her ex did a number on her, and she was committing to one single bravest acts I've seen anyone in her spot do... run like hell from an abusive prick of an ex to save her child.

It doesn't happen enough.

I proposed. No ring, no flowers, no fancy suit or dinner... only my wits to weave together a promise I hoped would be enough to convince her. I asked her to marry me with only the words I could muster in the moment and she said yes. I actually felt excited, kissing her for what was the first time as I held her in the air. She was squeezing me tighter than she ever did the entirety of her stay. Were we fixed on becoming something more? Maybe, if her life was taken from her by her ex. It's my understanding she did put up a fight but it wasn't enough. Her and the baby died. The ex was later shot by police, likely high out of his mind.

The upcoming Paris trip was supposed to be for the both of us.

MARCH 26 - APRIL 2, 2016:

While on a trip through Paris and Rome, a couple of interesting incidents took place. I remember flashes of being in a spaceship but something else entirely took place that is noteworthy. Well... two things happened that made Paris enjoyable, but a gentleman doesn't kiss and tell. It was just nice to connect with someone after losing my fiance, even if small amounts of alcohol may have been involved from the dinner we had together. I suppose I should count myself lucky she still looked as attractive as I remembered from the night before.

Dakota in Montaparnesse Tower, Paris, France

A couple nights into Paris, I was mostly unimpressed with the area and realized why "Paris Syndrome" is a thing. My group convinced our tour guide to drop us off at a riverboat cruise that would take us by the Eiffel Tower. The night was a bit chilly, and during the cruise it had started to rain so most had tucked themselves away to the lower deck of the boat, leaving the topside all to myself. As we approached the Eiffel tower, I felt a tap on my shoulder as if I was standing in the way of someone's photo. I went to step aside, quickly glancing over my shoulder to apologize, and had to give a second look seeing a familiar face. My deceased grandfather, standing next to my daughter Olivia. You can imagine my surprise being that it was just over three months since he passed away. He looked similar to his younger self that I've seen in old pictures, but there were also differences that seemed out-of-place. Meaning there were features that seemed a bit excessive for distortions in an old analog photo... But the bigger question was... what the heck was he doing with my daughter?

Obviously, the million questions running through my head were far from enough to take away the enjoyment of seeing them. I asked them what they were doing there, to which my grandfather replied that I was on the road to where I needed to be and that their guidance wasn't needed anymore. They might pop-in from time to time just to check in, which they both have done, but it became time for me to take the reigns of my life. My grandfather muttered something just before he left.

He said he was proud of me.

When in Rome, I had much more excitement in me. The ancient history, the views, the food... it was a much more fun experience overall. I opted in for a "Dinner with Tenors" optional event, and boy it did not disappoint. My first time really drinking alcohol, I figured if there was ever a good time to satisfy my curiosities it would be while I was on vacation and not gonna drive anytime during.

Dakota Singing on Stage at Dinner with Tenors

Vatican City - A tour Guide's Umbrella Visible - circa. 2016

While at the dinner I let it slip to some of the others that went with me I did a bit singing, and could play a bit of piano by ear. Upon hearing this, and hearing that the performers may invite people on stage, there was a heavy push to try getting me up to sing along. Eventually, after a birthday cake was brought out for a guest at another table and the champagne unleashed my inner opera singer... I was invited on the stage to help close the show.

Even the trip into Vatican City was filled with this energy about it. If walls could talk... it would be astounding to hear what those walls would have to say. Plenty controversy surround the Vatican, especially in the circles of conspiracy and occult. But it almost felt like somewhere... there was something tied to me lingering in the ether.

But.. what?

JUNE 2016:

I had a bit of a panic attack with news I had received. The woman I had a one-night stand with in Paris reached out to me through my website. She had noticed her body seemed off and took a pregnancy test that said she was positive. Too anxious about my reaction, she reached out to me wanting to schedule a video call to talk about things one-on-one, as she had felt with her lifestyle she didn't have too many people in her corner that would be supportive. I was hesitant to even tell anyone, already suspecting the snaky comebacks about, "not using protection," "she's just scamming you," etc... etc...

What attracted me to her was the fact we were both trying to be entrepreneurial types. And despite what influencers on social media make it out to be, that kind of lifestyle is lonely. Not many people want to associate with you, especially if you actually start to gain traction. It's hard work, mentally draining, and remarks of a clueless public can push one over the edge if a mental fortitude isn't developed.

AI Depiction of Dakota's Parisian Love Affair

No one wants to admit how many people who go down this road try to take their own life.

I wanted to wait for more facts to come forward before I said anything to my family, but this was to big! Was this it? Was the daughter I was looking for the byproduct of some exotic love affair? How would I support her and the kid? Would one of us have to move countries? Part of me wishes I kept silent but I had to get this out of my system because I just couldn't focus.

A couple days went by, and -censored-reached out to me yet again with updates from the doctor... it was a false positive. She had the onset of ovarian cancer triggering the false positive on the pregnancy test. Thankfully her options were open for treatment and she managed to beat it, meeting someone new along the way.

MARCH 13 - MARCH 14, 2017:

Last minute preparations for the Thailand venture have started with slight interference due to my debit card being compromised by some jackass in Florida using it to pay off court fines. Real ironic... I got the emails that my card had been declined and I did as I was supposed to in order to stop further usage. Three attempts were made on the 13th and a fourth attempt on the 14th. Only one charge was reflected in my account. Being my bank statement reflected a court payment service ran in Florida, I was able to quickly find some contact information on the firm in hopes it will help push things forward. I also made a note with my bank to let them know further contact may be difficult as I will not be in the country and just checking my emails might be an issue pending our hotel wifi signals.

MARCH 16, 2017:

-censored- was invited to -censored- birthday party on the 11th, and my mother finally mentions what -censored- had to say about what had taken place during the freeze out I had placed on my paternal family. She mentions that her asthma is triggered every time she is in contact with her mother, my stepmother, because of the drugs. This will be my ticket in to finally bring punishment. I will need to test my siblings for contact high... I have opened back up communications in order to get my reestablish the mission as I have caused enough confusion to mask my true intentions. If this is successful, I may lose my family, but it will be for the best. I can't keep doing this dance.

~~censored~~ had once again came to try and instigate an altercation, all because I was the one who got his brother arrested. This likely getting him banned from the store. I notified management to keep an eye on him. Whether or not they choose to listen is their folly. I am not really concerned about him, because my Thailand adventure is ever so close!

MARCH 18-20, 2017:

Finally the Thailand trip is among me. I had a long travel day ahead, from leaving town early to avoid the traffic and a potential call in from any one of my jobs to the flights and long layovers. This trip will take me through San Francisco and Hong Kong before finally reaching Bangkok. Since our group was spread throughout the entire state of Idaho we all had different meetup locations. We were split into two groups, one that gathered at Spokane the other was to meet up in Boise. I was in the Boise group. All in all there were 24 of us in total.

I had utilized my resources to at least get an idea of who I needed to look for while we were all gathering for our eventual meetup in San Francisco. I only knew 4 people from my past tours, which makes for an easy ride in but usually for someone in my

White Elephant Statue in Bangkok, Thailand

position I would like to have somewhat of an idea of who I am going to be with for these excursions. Utilizing email addresses attached to our group leader's messages I was able to track down just one face, -*censored* -. It wasn't until everyone had finally arrived at the Boise airport, that was supposed to, I was able to start reading everyone.

The group dynamic seems to be a good one. Several of the kids didn't travel alone, if they did they didn't take much time to find someone to bond with. It is a good measure. So far I have only identified 4 possible problem children should an incident take place; all of which seem to suffer from mental complications that even put stress on their parents. One shows nervousness when in one location for very long and complains about people taking pictures of him without consent (which is only irritating since gigs like this require both), and the others just show possible signs of autism. I try not to judge, and profiling is just a habit that never turns off once you've walked a similar path to my own.

Upon arrival in San Francisco we located our group leader, who tried to meet us at a rendezvous point. Those who were with him at the Spokane group were already waiting at our next gate. We had managed to make it this far without incident, except for a young lady, -censored-, mistaking a random stranger for our group leader from behind and proceeded to sneak up behind him. I will vouch that the man did bear a striking resemblance but her approaching the matter like that could have easily instigated a hostile situation. With threats of possible ISIS attacks and the methodology showing anyone with authority issues as likely to be "recruited," I must stay alert.

Once everyone was settled, we played card games and charged our electronics to pass the time. From San Francisco to Hong Kong was an over 12 hour flight (along with the 6 hour layover) I was both crammed on and was barely able to get to sleep. I managed to get in about 2, maybe 3, hours in as well as a few 10 minute naps spread in between. From Hong Kong to Bangkok was easier to manage as it was only about 3 hours.

In Bangkok we crossed paths with a group out of New Jersey who was, I believe, actually on their way back home after one more stay. My Idaho based group seemed to have been all placed on the same floor, so in the event of an incident I can reach most of them in a timely manner. All of them don't seem to possess much self defense skill, some only do so when provoked. I may have to utilize them.

Dakota standing in front of a temple

Once we got settled into our hotel room we were supposed to meet up to visit a nearby shopping area to get some food since meals were not covered for our first night in town. Unfortunately for me, I had overslept my alarm. In my defense I was hardly able to get any sleep on the way over here and the second I got into a shower, and was able to relax, my sleep deprivation took over.

Unfortunately for me, I got too comfortable to the point my nightmares started to rear their ugly head. This time it was a plane crash back on US soil, and kept with the theme of not being fast enough to save an innocent. I woke up as the bodies were burning.

MARCH 21, 2017:

It appears one member of my travel group has already come down with illness. One of the girls seemed to have contracted a strain of the flu virus before reaching here and it decided to make its move last night while they visited the shopping mall. We let her rest at the hotel and her condition seems to be improving, but as expected she is nervous around our more exotic food choices. In just hearing one has succumb to illness, though made obvious the manner of infection was different, my nerves have been set on edge as well.

Regardless, I cannot let it ruin a good trip. Earlier today we paid a visit to both the Grand Palace and Emerald Buddha Temple. The scenery of the area is absolutely breathtaking, though the weather that accompanies it has managed to fire areas of my skin. Seeing the Temple was reminiscent to my visit to the Sistine Chapel last year; as there were many guards to enforce the rules of No Photography/Video, No Shoes Inside, and Being Quiet. The first 2 rules I mentioned were readily enforced, as exhibited by two individuals the

A View of the Grand Palace in Bangkok

guards made delete photos they took on the inside. The quiet, they were lenient on.

Following the Holy Site visits, we walked to a taxi boat service and enjoyed a ride on the Chao Phraya River. Many local residents have homes along the riverbank, and a view of architectural sites really gave the place a historic feeling. Plus, getting to feed some catfish in the river itself was an interesting experience. After the boat ride, we had lunch at a nearby buffet, before we went back to the hotel for a couple hours.

-censored- girl who felt ill finally made an appearance before our dinner with "classical Thai dances." It was good to see her up and moving, but as mentioned before she wasn't up for trying anything really exotic. She mostly had water, and a couple pieces of watermelon. Chatter among the group shows she may have tried to eat too much at one point, aggravating her condition. I guess we just have to learn the hard way sometimes.

Sounds like another has been found ill, likely due to not being used to the conditions of the area. She, her siblings, and their (maybe) mother opted out of the dinner, seemingly due to motion sickness. Though… she didn't seem to have much trouble with our flights into the area since they were fairly turbulent… It should be noted the second child succumb to illness is one of the "problem" ones I mentioned before.

MARCH 22, 2017:

Another temple visit was done today as my group enjoyed a nice bus ride to the Grand Summer Palace. Shade from the many gardens helped keep us cool for the majority, as we checked out the architecture inspired by Chinese styles. Afterwards we stopped briefly for shopping before going on a tram ride into a historical area... truthfully I can barely understand our tour guide and it was hard to hear due to noise. The scenery continued to impress, and an elephant ride vendor was also nearby.

After, we had a buffet lunch and boat ride along our way back to Bangkok and to our hotel. I have actually been impressed with the local cuisine, enjoying it much more then I was anticipating thanks to warnings of Monkey Ball Soup. So far there has yet to be an incident similar to Xi'an, which I hope is how it stays for the rest of the trip.

MARCH 23, 2017:

Last night was our semi-last night in Bangkok. We will have one more night on our last day. But today, we took our bus from Bangkok to Kanchanaburi. On the way, we stopped at the Death Railway museum, the Floating Market, and a brief visit to a Coconut Plantation.

The coconut plantation was a rather interesting experience, as it not only harvests local vegetation but it houses several cool animals. According to our tour director ~~censored~~ some of the animals serve as important help on the plantation but are very well treated. There were squirrels, fighter fish, some catfish, eels, gibbons, and a large python (who looked like he had just had a good lunch). The tour company that arranged this trip tries to monitor local attractions to make sure everything will be safe for their travelers and the companies run like they should so no danger was there. I was also able to pick up a couple souvenirs here.

A view along the klong ride

The Market was an interesting experience. We rode there on a 20min klong ride, which took us through the backyard of many residents. We stopped at the market itself, which had many cool souvenirs but nothing that caught my interest. -censored- recommended we try a mango sticky rice that was sold there, and trying to be a bit more adventurous on this trip I had some. As we were trying to get it though, an older woman ambushed me with a massage using Tiger Balm. The massage sucked and my too damn kind travel face got me into buying four of the stupid things; which I am going to have to toss because I won't be able to take them on the plane. It won't be a waste of money since the exchange rate here is amazing coming from US dollars. 1 Thailand Baht is roughly 3 cents in US dollars.

Afterwards was the Death Railway museum housed information from Japanese WW2 POW camp information. The sites depicted were truly heart wrenching, for the normals. Ever start to wonder, whether the horrible things that happened will repeat.

~~censored~~ stayed close to me for most of this trip, often saying she's "seeking safety in tall people."

The hotel the company hooked us up in Kanchanaburi is absolutely amazing. It is a resort located right on the river bank, and it is not far from the controversial Tiger Temple. Our guide said the resort itself translated to "Sweet Honey Bee." I honestly wouldn't mind if I were stranded here for a while, there is plenty to do; two pools, an archery course, paintball & bb gun course, bicycle and ATV rentals, a deer park, a nice outdoor restaurant, and plenty of scenery to enjoy while on a hike. The wildlife here and fantasy decorations make for nice touch ups. Hell, there was Spider-man hanging out by the restaurant.

MARCH 24, 2017:

A wonderful day outdoors, with a river swim, train ride, and a hike down Hellfire Pass. It wasn't planned to necessarily be too much of an educational day, but more of a fun day in the tropics for the kids. I will have to admit, the river was a little intimidating as someone who sinks better then he swims; but, I am proud of myself for doing it. The boat took us up river, past a small waterfall, and dropped us off at a calm point. We were all required by law to wear a life vest (surprisingly they had one that fit me) due to the current having a reputation for taking tourists underneath some of the boats and them not making it out. The danger factor, was somehow appealing to me. The danger in itself didn't really arise till trying to get back on the boat as the current was getting worse AND trying to rip off my shorts! We took one of our group photos in the mentioned waterfall.

The next item on the list was a ride on the Death Railway, a train system built by Japanese POWs. It was quite an interesting ride through some of Thailand's mountain system. A huge plethora of tropical jungles, monkeys, and other exotic animals I was hardly able to photograph. Oh well, the elephants are coming up soon enough.

Dakota Toughing Out A Freezing Waterfall

Hellfire Pass was an interesting hike. It contained some remnants of the original tracks from the Death Railway. Memorials to British and Australian POWs were along the path. A new display was actually being built at the bottom of the trail, but it looked like it would be a couple months before it was finished.

MARCH 25, 2017:

Today was a transfer day as we drove further into the Thai countryside. The bus ride was long, and uncomfortable due a tailbone injury I sustained at the last hotel; keeping up with some of these kids is literally injuring me. Our first stop was at another temple, which was known for it's fortune telling and "make-a-wish" activities. Naturally, I tried my hand at both. The fortune telling was setup to operate like this: place a coin into a slot that corresponds to the day of the week one was born, wait for the spinning roulette light to stop on a number, then take a piece of paper the corresponded to that number. Mine landed on number 1 (naturally) and, according to the translation from our tour director, my fortune involved "dreams coming true, always stay in good health, lucky in love but not in gambling."

The "make-a-wish" was a bit more like a prayer ritual. One had to pay 20 baht for a bell they can write their name on, ring the bell, then make the wish facing a giant Buddha statue. My wish was to simply have everyone in my family find the answers they've been looking for and for a peaceful ending for what is to come. I know it probably defeats the entire purpose of the wish having jotted it down in these pages, but it is still worth mentioning.

One of the Final Lunches in Thailand

After the temple, we drove for another 2 hours till we reached our lunch reservation at a nice little resort. The layout of that resort was a lot more reminiscent of the river at home, but it was not the last stop. There was a pepper plantation near the resort, which lead up to our director suggesting we try the fried chicken. Like much of the Thai cuisine I've had a chance to try out while over here, I actually quite enjoyed it.

From lunch, we went straight to our hotel which lead to may of us diving straight for the pool when we got settled. I am sure going to miss these kids, and I should try to keep in touch with all of them when this is all over. There is already talk of meeting again on my old teacher's next trip, Scotland and Ireland.

MARCH 26, 2017:

The end trip depression has begun. Everyone has the "excited to go home but sad to leave here" mentality. I try to keep reminding them that the best things to do are to plan the next trip and keep in touch with one another.

Anyway, we visited an umbrella factory today. They made the old school straw umbrellas that typically aren't seen outside of performances in the modern day. Several painters were there that offered to design anything given to them, Hell you could have them paint your face if you wanted to. After a tour, and a stop in the market, some of the kids tried to convince me to get painted on my head after seeing a photo displayed of an older gentleman (with a similar hairline to my own) doing the same. I pointed out to them that the heat and humidity may screw up the look, and that our tour director mentioned where we liked to hit the pool every chance we got would have the same effect, so we settled on getting my camera case done. It was only 100 baht, which is a little less than 3 USD.

Dragon Design I had put onto Camera Case

After the Umbrella factory, we had a short stop at a silver factory which showed us a brief tutorial on how to spot real silver before we were able to do some shopping. I walked around a bit, checking out some of the designs that were available, but didn't buy anything due to most of the people I would buy for would probably ruin them.

After dinner, our tour guide hooked us up with a Took Took ride. We were in Chiang Mai at the time, and our drivers actually started to challenge one another. We had 3 stops, two at markets and by the US embassy, and our last stop naturally being our hotel. My friend ~~censored~~ and I rode together the entire time, and our driver happened to be the one who pushed the others into the race to show us a good time; though one of the drivers happened to rear end a car on the way through.

Dakota and Friend after Took Took Ride

MARCH 27, 2017:

As I have grown tired with the long days that seemed to be a poor attempt to extend our trip, I have forgotten to keep this journal updated as I went on. It is through photos I took that I am able to jot down the rest of my trip, so the exact days may be slightly off.

Dakota's Proof He's as Big as an Elephant

This was the day we were all waiting for, the day we got to play with the elephants! Early in the morning, we took off for an Elephant Sanctuary, as our tour director was able to have our group in particular get to stay a couple hours longer than originally planned which made everyone in the group very excited. We were instructed to bring our swimming suits, and a change of clothes, as our activities would include bathing with the elephants. On top of feeding, and just being in the presence of these beautiful animals, was an absolutely amazing experience. The elephants themselves were apparently quite mischievous, especially the 18 month old Tum-Took. There was a warning about getting too close to the baby, as he liked to squeeze people from behind, usually going for around the neck. -censored- furthered this warning by showing us a picture of him in that very situation. Tum-Took wasn't trying to hurt anyone, he just wanted to play.

Dakota just a few seconds away from wrestling an elephant over sugar cane

After our time with the elephants, it was time to go to lunch at a butterfly and orchid farm. All of our lunches were buffets, and as I mentioned before, the food was surprisingly delicious.

MARCH 28, 2017:

Last day in Chiang Mai, the post travel blues definitely settling in among the group. We had a couple more activities to check out just to get our minds off the end of the trails. *censored* are all feeling it pretty heavy, but we're doing what we can to embrace the last moments, and keep in touch once we were forced to walk our separate ways.

I think I might have to do a book dedication in their honor. ~~censored~~ actually gave me his email, so I can actually send him a free digital copy of it to prove it.

Anyway, our first stop was Kayaw Karen long neck tribe. ~~censored~~ handed us out biscuits to give to the tribe's children. They must've received a lot of tourist because they had several shops with nicknacks and a few other activities. They even had an option to test fire a crossbow. Our tour buses couldn't make it to where the tribe was located, so we had to hitch a ride in Thai taxis, which were similar to transport rigs for troops.

Afterwards we visited one more temple, the Grand Palace. The monks provided fortune telling, Holy Water blessings, and the monastery had a gorgeous view of Chiang Mai (if the fog wasn't there). It was quite interesting to see the many statues, and the history was always an interesting read. I never understood why but cultures with many thousands of years of background history always appealed to my interests. The Romans, most Asian cultures, things of that nature.

Kayaw Karen Tourist Sign

We ended the day with a trip to the nearby shopping mall. I did notice that sex trafficking warnings were posted all over, so those who knew my connections understood why I did what I did. I had suspicions the girls were being watched, so I did what I could to discreetly get the individuals watching the to turn away.

That night we didn't go back to our hotel for long, as we were scheduled to fly from Chiang Mai, back to Bangkok. Because it was a domestic flight, all of us had to check in our bags. Once in Bangkok, we were going to have a brief dinner at the first hotel we stayed at and head straight for bed. Before I could fall asleep, my own post travel blues hit me hard. I started crying about leaving the group... I was just going to miss everyone okay?!

-censored- brought around copies of the first group photo, actually setting off the post travel blues even more. I found myself saying the photo itself to feel empty because it was the day -censored- had to stay at the hotel since she was sick, ironically it was also the reason I felt like I need to watch over her.

MARCH 29-31, 2017:

We checked out of our hotel extra early so we could have a couple hours to relax and find our way around the airport. -censored- wasn't able to join us, but made sure to get photos with all of us as we got checked in. I made sure to get one, in case I wasn't able to find him so he and I could keep in touch. -censored- and my old teacher said they would try to find each other online, and I can use that connection to find -censored-

The flights, were naturally uncomfortable. We pretty much followed the same path we took into the country, on our way out. From Bangkok, we hung out for a few hours in Hong Kong. There -censored- wandered around the airport to find a good shop to get something to eat. -censored- recommended a fried prawn dish at the joint we settled on. Little did we realize, we ran short on time and had to scarf down our meals. Fearing our time was running even shorter, we ended up sprinting across the airport. Of course we only rushed to sit for an almost 13 hour flight to San Francisco.

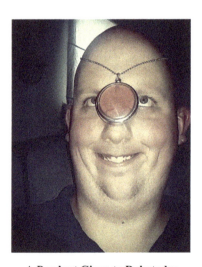

A Pendant Given to Dakota by One of the Monks

San Francisco was the point the Spokane and Boise groups were set to split up, but since we had at least 7 hours before flying out we took some time to hang out before going our separate ways.

Since the Spokane group was set to leave, those of us in the Boise group decided we might as well head to our gate. I confided in -censored-, just to get the feelings off my chest, as we waited at the gate. I could feel the trip slipping away from me, so I naturally turned to some comfort food to ease my stomach.

When we got on the plane home, I was stuck on a window seat. It was only a couple more hours till I was back into Boise and would have to say goodbye to everyone else. We arrived shortly before 10:30 at night,

Onboard Screen Showing View from Underneath the Plane

and I was met at the exit by my mother and grandmother. Before we left the airport, I snuck over to baggage claim to give a few more last goodbye hugs to everyone. After the drive home, I did not arrive till shortly after 1:00 am on the 31st.

I should note one of the mother's on the trip, who I confessed about my post travel depression settling in compared my situation to soldiers coming home after getting close to others in their unit. So the cliche "walls around my heart" have to be put up, and I have to maintain a certain attitude, to protect myself so I can keep going and reach out to more people.

When I started traveling, an interesting phenomena took place... the walls came down. The protective instincts my life has given me, and my training, stay there but the walls find openings within themselves and allow others in.

APRIL 12, 2017:

Not much has been taking place since I got back to reality. A fugitive that caused a chase was apprehended, no updates on the racial incidents mentioned in the last posting, not much to mention. One of my friends from my day job is leaving, but nothing too special. This is more of a reflective posting...

I meditated on images from Thailand, as some of my automatic writing sessions indicated I saw this venture coming and it somehow may be linked to Olivia. I swore I've had dreams showing me in lush tropical areas identical to areas I visited in Thailand. Something was watching me, someone very similar in appearance to one of the girls in my travel group. At least in passing...

APRIL 23, 2017:

It's been nearly a month since my return from Thailand, and there have been some noteworthy developments. In my social circles, -censored- also seems to have ceased communication after learning about my enrollment in a private investigation course. Despite being a friend, he sometimes shows envy as I progress in life. He acknowledges my strategic approach but his actions suggest some underlying discontent, personal conversations about what's been going on in his life, however... show that I've been blind to what he's been going through.

I AM THE SPECIALIST OF THE STRANGE | 121

Moving on, I plan to reach out to censored this week to obtain censored. They showed interest in the Scotland and Ireland trip, especially censored, who seemed fascinated by the tales of leprechauns and fairies. My experience in paranormal investigation might pique her interest.

In family matters, a disagreement erupted between my mother and me when I shared my candid opinion on escorting censored to her school play, which I found lackluster.

AI Depiction of Dakota Realizing Friend's Struggles

censored was prevented from performing during school due to a sudden drop in her grades, and I believed she should have been excluded entirely. Further discussion uncovered her aggressive behavior towards other students, which my mother dismisses, likely because it supports my apparent "hostility."

In my pursuit of crime fighting, I've applied to the censored to further validate my investigative skills and promote my business. My application is pending, and once accepted, the program should take 3 to 6 months to complete. I plan to finance my studies independently, eager to engage with material that will be of practical use.

Regarding the arts, I'm considering a strategy to increase music sales. My distributor recently introduced a licensing feature, allowing for legal cover song distribution. My plan is to weave unrelated songs into a narrative, starting with "Desperado" by the Eagles, "Hurt" by Nine Inch Nails, and "I Don't Want To Miss A Thing" by Aerosmith, crafting a tale of an outlaw caught in a relentless cycle of love and loss.

My upcoming book, "The Ones Who Walk All Worlds: Lover's Cry Part 2," is taking shape after overcoming a severe case of writer's block. It's currently focused on the perspective of the love interest from "A Giant's Curse," and I'm curious to see how the story will unfold.

MAY 3, 2017:

I've been accepted into a program that's set to bolster my business and potentially shape my career. Interestingly, my law enforcement activities garner less public skepticism, perhaps due to my presence. The program has already proven beneficial, offering resources for new equipment and investigative techniques. I'm confident in my choice; it allows me to self-fund my education, learn subjects that fascinate me outside the standard curriculum, and leverage my innate skills. With the rise in infidelity, drug crimes, and general folly, I could very well establish my enterprise locally.

This path, however, presents its own set of challenges, but I believe I have some solutions. Like all my endeavors, I must approach each step as a strategic risk, planning for as many contingencies as possible.

Prioritizing car maintenance is key for me right now to extend its life. It seems the car needs minor fixes, like an alignment and a hub bearing replacement, which are manageable for a car-savvy person, unlike myself. On the bright side, a substantial paycheck from my day job, including overtime, is on its way to cover these costs. I've also paused the automatic payments for my Scotland and Ireland trip to free up some funds.

On another note, my t-shirt fundraiser for seed money hasn't been successful, so I'm considering it solely for charity now. However, I've discovered stock brokerage as a potential funding source. I'm exploring a platform that allows investing in stocks with any budget. I plan to maintain my day job for financial security while I navigate this new venture. I've already invested in a film studio called ~~censored~~ whose recent movie ~~censored~~ has been well-received. Although it's not showing in Idaho, I'm awaiting its DVD release and considering increasing my investment as the studio gains more recognition.

Either way, things are about to get interesting.

As it stands, I'll need to adjust my various projects accordingly:

IN Music - I'm putting a hold on the cover song plans for now. I might consider doing a single song to accompany future book releases as a thematic element, but that requires further exploration.

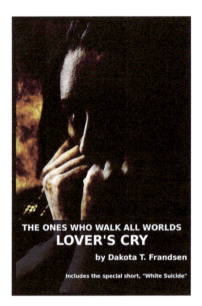

The Ones Who Walk All Worlds: Lover's Cry Cover

IN Books - I'm aiming to establish a new daily routine that includes at least 30 minutes to an hour of writing to meet the increasing demands. I plan to pause work on "The Ones Who Walk All Worlds" after releasing "Lover's Cry Part 2," to explore other genres. Although I started designing a title for this journal last night, it seems this task will have to be postponed.

IN Movies/Television - I've decided to remain off-camera for the time being. I'm looking to delve deeper into an investigative role, which I believe will yield plenty of fresh material for screenwriting. I'm open to making cameo appearances if opportunities present themselves, but for now, I'll continue with my usual approach.

IN Gaming - I attempted to launch a gaming channel on YouTube, but I've decided to drop that endeavor and keep gaming solely as a stress reliever. Holding onto my childhood favorites should help maintain a clear mind.

IN Travel - There are no planned changes here unless a major conflict arises. The experiences are too enriching to give up, and the travel company I use consistently delivers engaging adventures. The upcoming Scotland and Ireland trip will likely be my last with the high school group. The tour company offers various programs tailored to different age groups, and after my next European trip, I'm considering joining the "College Break" tour, designed for 18-28-year-olds. While I enjoy chaperoning the younger crowd, it's time I travel with peers closer to my own age.

May – June 2017

I'm being stalked at work, tires slashed twice. All because I told a guy I thought was a friend a baby his fiance was pregnant with was not his child. It didn't take much to figure out he was involved, the fucking moron needs his head bashed in for how stupid he's acting, but he's not exactly thinking with the head on his shoulders.

MAY 12, 2017:

A scumbag I have been monitoring for the past few months has committed vandalism today and I was the target. As I was working at my day job, I received a phone call from my mother stating ALL of my tires were flat and I needed to get outside immediately. I was able to clearly see the entry wounds on all tires, but another thing caught my attention; a familiar face was watching me from a truck. The suspect's boyfriend, an old friend of mine from High School, drives an older model red pick up truck with a large American flag sticking out of the bed of it... the suspect was watching me from a vehicle by the same description. I am going to pester the managerial staff at my day job until they let me see the tapes, just so I can confirm my suspicions. The woman probably thinks she would get away with it since she is set to enter a guilty plea come Monday.

AI Depiction of Dakota's Tires Being Slashed

Jesus, my friend is pathetic moron for wanting to stick with this chick.

Motives for the actions likely stemming from me egging my friend on about alleged pregnancy news. My friend has admitted she has cheated on several occasions, purchased drugs from another suspect I have been monitoring, and I have caught her breaking into my friend's truck the last time they were together. It should be noted my friend is also suicidal, and the last time these two broke it off, he got very dark. But in light of recent events, I have classified him as "Stage 2- SI," SI standing for "stupid idiot."

Little do the outsiders realize I have a tendency to set up my targets to attack in order to get enough witnesses to throw out any speculation of innocence, and once again the system worked. I just have to tie the evidence together.

MAY 17, 2017:

On Mother's Day, my tires were slashed again, finally pushing forward the investigation as it was easy to determine this was a targeted attack. I was able to spot at least 3 possible suspects stalking the area as I was leaving my day job and passed the collected intel to the officer who took the case. I was also able to uncover that the tire department that worked on my car had a few other similar incidents take place over the last couple weeks. As I was speaking to the officer yesterday, I brought this up to see if she was aware of said incidents, but none came up. If my incident is indeed connected, I may have to approach this at a new angle.

At home my sister -censored- came home with an interesting invite from her school. One of her teachers is organizing a summer vacation trip for the 2019; going through Paris, Nice, Florence, Pisa, and Rome. The trip is organized through the company my last few trips have been through, so I already know she'd be in good hands. My mother has a stipulation she would need a chaperone with her to keep an eye on her. Naturally, -censored- leaned towards having me join her. She is at the age she won't want any relatives with her, but having her brother along who's been in the region and less likely to pressure her the entire time and actually let her have some fun is easily the more tolerable choice. There is a meeting next Wednesday I might try to sneak her too so she can actually get the information from someone she'll at least (pretend to) pay attention.

AI Depiction fo Dakota Taking His Sister to Her School

My mother tried to bar her from going, but a part of me wondered if getting to go on one of these exotic trips would do my sister some good to get her act together. I took her against my mother's wishes, with the only stipulation she keep out of trouble. One incident and it was done for.

A teaching moment? Perhaps, if my sister hadn't been caught yet again exploiting herself off to boys in her class. It probably worked out for the best... as I learned that the HR lady at my work goes on this trip every year.

MAY 18, 2017:

The management finally revealed surveillance photos to me, capturing the person who slashed my tires. I could just make out the culprit: a male in his early to mid-40s with a skater/gang look, foolish enough to shop right after his first offense. This shifts the case's strategy somewhat, but my immediate action was to apologize to my friend for my initial reaction, though not for my words. Interestingly, the suspect showed up again today, providing a chance to uncover his identity, and my friend obvious to the fact I watched him signally the suspect to get away.

The case is unfolding.

MAY 21, 2017:

The individual who has been targeting me has yet to make another appearance, which is probably the only smart thing he has done. I will continue to wait for the opportunity to get a photo of him, with other subjects in question. But, an interesting note should be made in the event it turns into something. A male in his early 20s was taken by ambulance to the hospital for a series of stab wounds, not much else was reported. It could be unrelated, but it could mean a confrontation among the group of suspects took place. The one who started this chain of events didn't show up for work today, when he looked just fine yesterday. I will need to continue to monitor the situation.

Regardless of how it unfolds, I still gotta keep going.

MAY 24, 2017:

I did some surveillance at my day job in order to hopefully spot the suspect who slashed my tires, but was unable to locate him. It seems my "friend" passed along the news I was looking into a gun and that the suspect was caught on camera. That only points it all to him even more. Managerial staff showed the photo to my uncle, however, and it should be noted deception in is the air. It appears my "friend" lied about the suspect's identity. I cannot say for sure yet, but it's an interesting development.

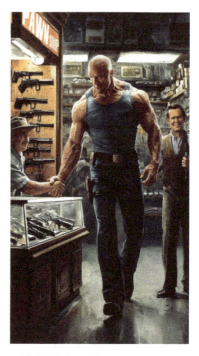

AI Depiction of Dakota Entering Pawn Shop

As for the weapon, I am looking into a EAA Witness 9mm pistol as my sidearm. I found one for a good price, and will be talking to an old friend at a local pawn shop to see if they can help with the arrangements. People should really stop underestimating how far I'll go to stand my ground, or the people who will only stop me to make sure I use the right tools to get the job done.

If you're gonna do something, you may as well be smart about it.

MAY 25, 2017:

I recently grabbed a copy of "LOGAN" after its home release. As a film industry enthusiast, I recognize its exceptional production, yet it stirs unique thoughts within me, especially following the tire incident.

Continuing down this path, I feel compelled to embody Wolverine—not just the battle-scarred loner, but the formidable weapon. I'm already the person who cares deeply, perhaps too much. It's now a matter of all or nothing. I need to delve deeper into learning—mastering firearms, blades, self-defense, martial arts, and advanced weaponry. I must grow stronger, quicker, wiser. I must confront my inner demons and prepare for battle. Wolverine is a part of my identity, integrated into my brand, but I aim to evolve into an unprecedented force. I must absorb wisdom from the greatest.

OCTOBER 31, 2017:

Rumors of a satanic cult in the area participating in animal sacrifices started to resurface again, possibly due to the fact it is Halloween. I do believe there is something to the rumors but as far as finding a tangible thread to take the threat on, that has proven difficult.

NOVEMBER 11, 2017:

AI Depiction of Satanic Cults Summoning an Evil Being

I contacted an old friend, who has bugged me about joining in on a hunt since I met him about 5 years ago to discuss the details of the time travel investigation to see if he could prove any more ideas to better improve the already slim chances of actually pulling off such a stunt. He didn't provide much input on that matter but brought up another situation he was dealing with that I might've been able to provide an assist. He believed he was being stalked by an entity known as the "Hat Man." Eyewitness accounts, including my own, describe him as a shadow person who appears to wear a trench coat and a fedora-like hat. Others include details of glowing red eyes, a suit, a briefcase, and even a cane.

Many people believe the "Hat Man," is a bringer of misfortune… that he likes to cause chaos. The truth is he simply can sense when someone is under heavy emotional stress, and likes to stir things up a bit. I have reason to believe the,

"Hat Man," was once human but was quite the asshole. I had a run in with him in my early days, right around the time I was dealing with my father's actions. It was through this encounter I was able to figure out how to get rid of him, which the advice I forwarded to him. Just tell the guy to piss off.

The exact specifics are much more difficult but it is the basic idea. The "Hat Man," is a supernatural bully so telling him to screw off is part of it but there are entire processes to completely eliminate supernatural threats like that. I may include something like a "paranormal encyclopedia" in the "Frandsen Files Initiative" when I finally get around to writing it (Maybe a sort of compendium, rather...)

7

Becoming the Specialist of the Strange

NOVEMBER 24, 2017:

Remains of ~~censored~~ found 3 weeks ago IDed, leak not has not been made public ~~censored~~. Turns out it belongs to a 2 year old missing persons case from a nearby county. Female, early 20s, reward money might be available, I may need to help dig into this under the circumstances.

Dakota, the Bounty Hunter

NOVEMBER 25, 2017:

Officially on investigation of -censored- located key details on events leading up to her death, first priority is to find the rest of her.

I can't shake the idea of -censored- from my mind, so I'm officially taking the case. I did a little background on the victim and was able to find a timeline of events leading up to the initial investigation. It appears two suspects are already in line; one being an ex boyfriend who fathered the lady's baby that didn't live past a month, and the other being a new fiance who is currently serving time for drug charges and evading police.

According to news reports, there was an altercation between the two gentlemen beforehand because the ex tried to convince her not to move in with new fiance. Further investigation already done revealed the victim's clothes were found at a spot in -censored- I have a few ideas, but nothing can be proved without -censored-

NOVEMBER 26, 2017:

I had a possible communication with the victim through dreamstate vision, it's looking like the spirit trying to make contact since the remains were found, guy who killed her already in prison, must find -censored-

NOVEMBER 28, 2017:

Scrying for -censored- barely turning up anything. I'm getting more and more of a bad feeling this is something more than just a love triangle turned fatal.

DECEMBER 2, 2017:

There was a shooting just moments before I pulled into the parking lot at my workplace. State police had set up a drug bust that had gone wrong, hoping to add more charged being that my workplace was across the street from one of the local high schools. One suspect attempted to run into the store to try hiding from police, not realizing the store had started locking its doors at midnight

A Horror Inspired Self Portrait

in response to theft. Both suspects apprehended, one shot and wounded by police.

December 23, 2017:

AI Depiction of Dakota Listening to the Recording

My aunt shared a voice recording from a psychic session where she claimed to hear my grandfather's voice. Intrigued, I conducted my own audio session and received a message urging me to stop bothering my aunt, eerily reminiscent of my late grandfather's voice.

Additionally, another voice emerged, claiming to be that of a missing girl whose skull was recently discovered. She expressed awareness of my search for her and indicated she's been attempting to lead me.

December 27th 2017:

Hitman request

A woman I was talking with on a dating website mentioned that she lived with abusive parents and would ask if I would kill her parents for her. Obviously I cut my ties right then and there. Whatever happened with her, I honestly have no idea... probably for the best that it stays that way. Seriously, how screwed in the head do you have to be to try getting some random guy online to murder your family. I discussed the situation with one of my police contacts and they said they'd look into it.

January 24th, 2018

Walls of Eden Sigil

Angel sigil experimentation.

Using sigils from the book "Angelic Sigils, Keys & Calls by Benn Woodcroft" and taking design elements from communication sigils from The Keys of Solomon I designed a protection sigil I dubbed "The Walls of Eden." The power of this thing would not be fully shown until years later.

March 19th-28th 2018

Earth → Scotland and Ireland Trip, Nessie and Crowley

My last trip with my travel group was a tour of Ireland and Scotland. My initial plan was not to go, however I quickly changed my mind upon learning the last stop on the trip was at Loch Ness, a location I always wanted to visit with the hopes of seeing Nessie. Part of my attention was diverted due to being in the middle of a breakup at the time but overall the trip was amazing.

St. Patrick's Cathedral - Dublin, Ireland circa. 2018

Before the day we rode out to Loch Ness, we visited spots through Ireland and Scotland, I remember brief images of seeing craft in the sky. I would also get views of the landscape as if I was on board the aforementioned ships. One such instance I was taken above the waters of Loch Ness days before our group made the official trip and was shown the high concentrations of quartz in the region.

When we got to the Loch, my eyes never left the water. And to my surprise a large aquatic animal breached the surface as it was trying to avoid a black speedboat. I did my best to capture photos, with only two showing the large object in the water but nothing that clearly defined what it was.

Dakota's Reflection next to 3D Recreation of Robert Burns

I AM THE SPECIALIST OF THE STRANGE | 143

**Screenshot of Mirror Article
Discussing Dakota's Sighting**

I reported my sighting to the Loch Ness Registry when we got back to the hotel and the story started to go a bit viral as I was on the plane ride home. I also came to learn that I may have had supernatural assistance from my great grandmother who passed from old age roughly an hour before my arrival at Loch Ness.

The following pages will show up close potential photos of "Nessie." It was the best I could get under the circumstances, but regardless of suepernatural assistant or not getting something on the first attempt, when others can go decades with nothing to show for it, is impressive. The ordeal managed to capture the attention of producers for a National Geographic special called "Drain the Oceans."

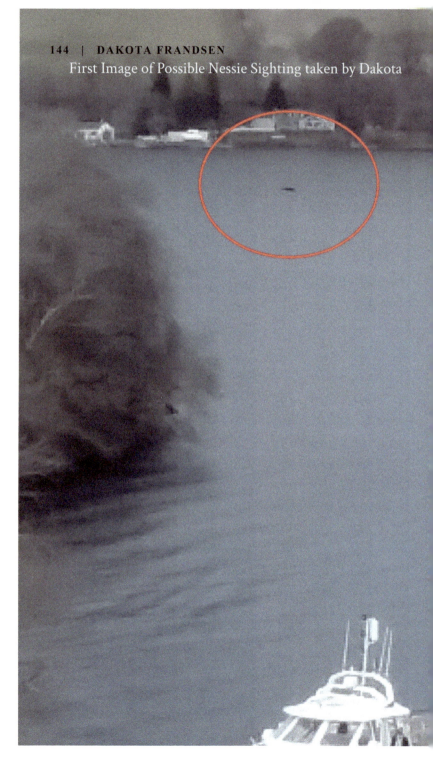

First Image of Possible Nessie Sighting taken by Dakota

Second Image of Nessie Sighting taken by Dakota

While getting ready to leave Loch Ness, we caught a view of Aleister Crowley's house where I swore I could see a cloaked figure watching us. For lack of better word the figure looked similar to a KKK member cloak. If that was mister Crowley... I'd be more intrigued to explore this without children hanging about me.

November - December 2018

After a YouTube channel called -censored- (one involving the family of the missing woman) tells a couple incidents involving me, I was reached out to by a gentleman who believed he may be possessed by a large demon dog-like being, one that had him enter a blood contract while in a dream-state.

What caught my interest was the claim that upon waking from the dream, the client claimed that his hand was completely torn apart as if he just smashed a window. Even more disturbing was the claim of animals behaving oddly, as if they were frightened by an apex predator.

AI Depiction of Vapula Trying to Kill Dakota

The nudges in my gut told me to take this case, something was genuine. Further developments identified the being as Vapula. All methods to try dealing with the situation remotely were not working, this incident was going to have to require a personal session. Very quickly it escalated into a violent exorcism that nearly came to spontaneous combustion, the man's skin started to blister as if he was exposed to extreme heat. Eventually the being broke the connection, escaping the room as a dark mass before proper bindings could be completed. For now, the kid was safe. To this day I'm not sure what lured this thing to the kid. There weren't signs of drug use, abuse, alcohol, nothing of the sort. Mostly this was a kid stressed out over college exams.

About two weeks later, in a dream state, I was presented with a vision of walking through what looked like an abandoned internment camp with several years of overgrowth. As I was walking through it I could hear a radio playing what sounded like 40s music. I found a room with the radio on the floor and walked in. Immediately static broke through the music and I recognized it as something making contact. Towards the back of my head I felt another transmission trying to break through, warning me that this was a trap. Whoever was coming through the radio didn't seem to register the warning as it continued trying to taunt me. I demanded the being identify itself again, bringing up the cliche "in the name of Christ," line and that only pissed it off further.

The being jumped out of the radio, wrapping its hands around my throat, growling in a low and raspy voice, "It's Vapula bitch!" The next thing I knew I was pinned to the wall of my bedroom by my neck by a large shadow mass, and it was squeezing harder. This was no longer a dream...

I grabbed at this thing's hand, trying to let myself a few more breaths of air. Its "skin," felt like the leather of a manged animal. I managed to mutter the words, "Michael... help... now!" I could see this thing's face looking up at the ceiling in fear. The next thing I knew there was light shooting out of my eyes and mouth, Valpula just let out this huge squeal, similar to a herd of pigs being slaughtered at once. I quickly lost consciousness.

AI Depiction of Vapula's Ambush

The next morning I woke up on the floor and went to go outside to run out the garbage. My neighbor approached me asking what the heck was going on because something about my house was scaring the hell out of her dogs, she even mentioned seeing the light and hearing the screams of an animal being butchered. She was also knowledgeable about my supernatural endeavors, often joking I should be driving a '67 Chevy. That's when I noticed my neck still had red marks belonging to the hand of someone, or rather something, much bigger than myself. At the sight of the marks, my neighbor nearly had her eyes pop out of her skull. I just left it at, "It's better that you don't know. I'm hoping what it was, is done for," and went about my business.

The next few weeks chatter was quiet on the supernatural wavelengths, possibly figuring I was needing time to process what had happened. By the time someone came through, a male's voice told me that word quickly spread that I severely wounded Vapula, and there was a newfound fear of me. Angels, regular spirits... they knew about what I was and sometimes came across as being intimidated as the story spread. Apparently the "other side" is filled with gossip. Though intimidated, they knew I could be trusted. As for any "demonics," they would be scared to approach.

What the hell am I?

December 2019

The Hunt for Infinite Earths was underway. An experimental procedure to utilize simple ghost hunting methods, a bit of magic, and clever planning to make contact with beings from other worlds... possibly even "alternate Earths." I knew that it would be unwise to simply just leave an open invite, that simply invites too much risk and the situation over in China already is seeding enough misfortune for darker beings to be roaming about more freely. I anticipate this will only escalate.

AI Depiction of Archangel Metatron

In regards to the experiment, after some careful research, I have picked three potentially viable targets to focus on. Setting the intention on these individuals would help prevent interference. A part of me felt the need to get an outside assist in order to get the necessary strength to reach off world. An immediate instinct was to research lore surrounding angels, settling on Archangel Metatron for his insights to worldly happenings. It would seem the angel with a "true face" the size of the Earth would also have sights on alternate dimensions. I would learn later that the Metatron may in fact be a sort of natural frequency in line with Source... a direct line to all other frequencies.

As for my targets, I needed ones who had some sort of visitation or interaction with THIS Earth... and it be a previously documented case. Otherwise it increases the odds of infiltration. For this experiment I picked three individuals that would fit the bill nicely, if they were in fact real.

I AM THE SPECIALIST OF THE STRANGE | 151

1. Vrillon - An ET claiming to be connected to the Ashtar Galactic Command that hijacked Saturday morning cartoons in 1977 in the UK. Witnessed by hundreds
2. Val Thor - A Venusian who spent five years living in the Pentagon, Crew of five, including wife Jilian
3. John ~~censored~~ - A potential comic book character come to life, writers based character on really occult practices and swear to this day they have seen him out and about in the flesh

Each individual was carefully researched and selected on the fact their individual cases held multiple eyewitnesses, even some physical evidence of interaction in our world. That measure alone spoke to increased odds of interaction. By using Metatron as an interdimensional satellite dish, this in theory would allow stronger and more stable communication. What other rules did I have to consider? Hard to say, not like there's much of a manual on these things.

But here are corresponding the results:

AI Depiction of Dakota Contacting the Multiverse

1. If Vrillon could hear me, me let me go to voicemail... so to speak. I have come to learn years later that the Ashtar Galactic Command doesn't inter-

act with civilians, so it is quite possible that no interaction was because I was some random individual.
2. When contacting Val Thor the communications seemed a bit more active. Some audio tapes were erased, and a small spherical craft showed itself while I was visiting the local wind-farm with family, some following audio sessions done after the corrupted files were discovered indicated a hostile exchange but matters quickly settled
3. The strangest of it all. Faint audio sessions, voices matching the description of the character, but a single recording left through an anomalous source of static left a message stating clear as day "If you can hear me, ~~censored~~ wants you"

Much to my surprise, ~~censored~~ was the most successful contact, and he has made appearances on a few other instances when a case has turned south, offering up his skillset. I approached a couple of the writers involved with the original storylines, and they advised me to be careful as ~~censored~~ is not a man to be trusted and will screw me over the moment it benefits him.

March - April 2020

Earth - United States - Idaho → North Carolina

Gibbon Exhibit at Zoo Boise

As COVID lockdowns started to be enacted in my home state, I was asked to appear in a Paranormal Parody show called Conspiracy Cases. It was something a little different from my usual calls so I went ahead and made the drive. It was only two hours away and it gave me a chance to have a weekend away. Filming was only a few hours at an old bomb shelter in Boise and on my days off, no better time to do it.

Plus this gave me a chance to visit a local zoo, and go back to the Old Idaho State Penitentiary to revisit where I learned there was life after death. Being that I was on my own for the weekend, I wanted a chance to go visit some places in Boise I didn't normally get a chance to when I was with my family and the women just wanted to go shopping. I don't mind a shopping trip but there's so much more to do!

Dakota on Location for Conspiracy Cases

While I was deemed an "essential worker" and able to still work through the pandemic, I decided to start looking to making documentaries from home to hone my skills, and maybe try something new. Being I had personal interest in from previous encounters was brought to the forefront of my mind as a spike in reports of him making an appearance.

Figures that the world would go insane and he would emerge to watch it all unfold.

During my research, a post on Reddit made the comparisons between the *-censored-* to a being from Brenton mythology known as the Ankou, which is essentially a type of Grim Reaper. When I went down this rabbit hole, one of the origin stories for the Ankou was that the being was none other than the first born son of Adam and Eve. Cain, from Cain and Abel. When I read this, I could swear I heard a maniacal laughter.

Almost like something out of a movie, a phone call came through on a "hotline" I had briefly set up right as I was coming home at about 3 in the morning. A father out of North Carolina was frantically calling any paranormal-based groups and exorcists looking for help regarding a being that was focusing its attention on the man's then 3-year-old son. The second I heard on the voicemail that was left that a child was involved, I immediately called the father back.

AI Depiction of "The Call"

An almost four-hour conversation detailing nearly all the cliches (smells, scratches, voices, shadows, a "dead" room where life seemed to be drained by anyone who entered. ramped up in intensity when the voice of what sounded like a five year old boy say, "Put down the fucking phone or I'll kill you bitch."

Needless to say, I was fully convinced this was a legitimate call. I got more information from the father. He detailed that this being had apparently been around for a while, since the father was in his teens, and had been offering up a position as a "general of some army." Being that there was an obvious effort on the being's behalf to establish some kind of rapport, I asked the father if it ever said its name.

The father, not knowledgeable about biblical names, did not understand the significance of the name but I knew it well.

The being identified itself as Cain.

Cain slaying Abel

By Peter Paul Rubens - The Courtauld Institute of Art, London, Public Domain, https://commons.wikimedia.org/w/index.php?curid=28935710

Naturally, having the world's first murderer hanging around would be unsettling for anyone. I calmed the father and sent him detailed instructions to break the ties with Cain as he finished up the move. So far, no further incidents have been reported and the family is in a new house here in Idaho.

Within the same week of this revelation, a visitor appeared in my bedroom right as I was getting home from work. The time was just after 3am, I was pretty much just beat and heading straight for bed. As I walked into my bedroom I watched a woman walk out of what looked like a closing portal. Just feeling the energy coming off of her was overwhelming.

It wasn't that she was anything negative, in fact quite the opposite, she was very motherly... her frequency denoted that she was ancient. She identified herself as Eve, as in THE Eve from the Garden of Eden. She felt the need to show me something in relation to Cain, something she felt would help me understand who and what I was up against.

Eve placed her hand on my temple, instantly showing me the Garden of Eden through her eyes... Cain was not Adam's biological son... Adam knew it and was the first abusive stepfather... Cain was manipulated into killing his brother, siding over with darker forces... who was that he sided with?

He seemed familiar, almost identical to the "dragon man" I saw the day my stepmother stabbed me... that was so

AI Depiction of Eve's Arrival

long ago. Eve seemed to know me, know about me, know that I was someone who could probably help shift the tide... why?

Because, according to her, I was very similar to her son but became something better like she hoped he would.

November - December 2020

Close to Christmas, my grandmother and mother were trying to think of some kind of plan to get my younger cousin, -censored-, away from her mother. There have been disturbing hints of some nasty abuse taking place at the hand of my aunt's latest boytoy and alleged father of her two youngest children. They lived in -censored- at the time, about a three-hour drive from my location. Visits were rare. All I knew for sure was that my aunt's children were not making attempts at their own lives before the "stepfather" came in. Well, within 24 hours, -censored- called my grandmother and asked to come stay with her because her mother threw her into an insane asylum for saying her "stepfather" molested her and told -censored- that she could not come home.

This was after -censored- had reached out TWICE to get help because her mother was letting this piece of shit hurt her.

We get -censored-, we discover how much has been going on. -censored- reached out a couple times before to try telling us about the abuse pushing her to where she contemplated suicide, all messages forwarded to the authorities immediately. Conveniently I was "banned" from my aunt's shortly after. But the extent of what -censored- had revealed honestly made it so it was probably for the best I never saw my aunt again.

-censored- was released from the mental health facility for a two week break, which she spent at my house. Apparently it was meant to be a bit of a holiday for long-term patients so they can spend time with family and gather their things. My aunt didn't even let my cousin have that much. This whole mess was heartbreaking to watch.

When -censored- left, I was honestly heartbroken. She was the one of my cousins I was closest to, and knowing that someone deliberately let this happen would've made for any "crimes of passion" defense moot if I were to do something. I needed a distraction, something to get my mind off of how much -censored- needed help but I couldn't do anything. I got a notification on Twitter about an international paranormal group, -censored- looking for members, and figured what the hell. I signed up, quickly rose through the ranks, then… well… I witnessed a battle between literal Heaven and Hell.

8

This Was War

January 2021

My attempt at a documentary, "The Hunt for Olivia," was picked up by a new paranormal based streaming service, with added investigation footage. My attention was brought to this streaming platform by one of the former heads of "The Company" that had me helping him edit some investigation clips

The Hunt for Olivia Promotional Cover

for him. Working with this man lead to some conflicts, and

not knowing who to really trust in these matters I stepped away and pursued my own interests. Was it a smart move to make? Probably not, not much has been made from it but it's still good to get out and experiement.

February 14th-15th 2021

I was visiting a friend in Coeur d'Alene for Valentine's weekend. For ~~censored~~ I managed to get access to decent wifi so I could attend livestreams we did to promote the company. We'd talk about company updates, research cases, various forms of phenomenon, etc...

Mountains in Oregon, on the way to Coeur d'Alene

I was continuing my research for the ~~censored~~ documentary. ~~censored~~ was internationally based and gathered reports from all over the globe. Apparently a ~~censored~~ case had emerged prompting a company wide allocation of resources to uncover the truth. While on the livestream, it seemed that somebody wasn't happy.

Shadows racing around people, mysterious voices, growls, all started to scare the audience but it was far from the worst of it. Knowing I had experience against this thing, the CEO asked me to speak about my prevailing theory on the matter. When I said that the -censored- was Cain, the battle had begun.

In the UK, one of our members messaged me about a burning sensation around his throat and he was coughing up blood.

AI Depiction of UK Member Coughing Up Blood from Unknown Cause

Another member claimed that a huge gust of wind burst through his front door, followed by shadows and a deep cold dread sensation.

Texas, a woman claimed she saw three beings sizing her up. The skin around her throat seemed to compress as if an invisible hand was choking her.

West Virginia, another woman had a redness and shortness of breath around her throat.

Idaho, I started to feel a tingle up and down my spine, my system overloading. It honestly felt like I had a seizure. I had to disconnect to recalibrate myself. On the other screen I had up, I watched as more people dropped, leaving the three overwhelmed. As one of the guys, -censored- who remained started to suggest ending the stream, recapping the events, another gentleman, -censored- started to act strange. -censored- leaned towards his webcam, as if trying to stare "through the screen," immediately putting the fear into -censored-. If one had to describe the vibe coming from -censored- it would be best described as "I won, what will you do now?"

For a brief moment I noticed something. As -censored- went to mention my name, -censored- would flinch as if the very mention of me triggered a PTSD-esque response. -censored- said my name again and the same thing occurred. I may have had a way to end this. My issue was that -censored- had several small children in the house, and was on and off chemo, this could've gone south very quickly. But inaction was the only thing which guaranteed a worse outcome.

AI Depiction of the Possession

I left a message to "Let me in, I can end this," in the livestream chat as only two remained on the screen. -censored- had left, leaving -censored- with our -censored- at the time. -censored- was trying to get -censored- to speak but his words fell on deaf ears. My web connection held and I was able to step in. -censored- quickly showed fear but tried to hide it.

"I know who you are. I know what you want. Let. Him. Go."

AI Depiction of Dakota Getting Charged Up

-censored- slowly shook his head no.

"Now," my voice reverberated.

The being that took influence of -censored- broke the connection, but far from willingly. It took a few minutes for -censored- to gather himself and the livestream continued on.

Before the playtime began, I asked -censored- what he saw while he was under, to which all he said was "You already know."

End of February 2021

As progress was being made in helping heal those affected the worse by Cain's assault on -censored- there was a visitation from a rather unusual party. Potentially Lucifer himself. Lucifer seemed worried about one of the members most heavily affected by the assault, as well as the absence of the accompanying entity tied to this individual, who identified herself as Lillith. Lucifer was pleading for a favor, appealing to the side of me that had started to catch romantic feelings for ~~censored~~ to justify my taking part in what would amount to a rescue mission. Lilith had gone missing. ~~censored~~ was not even able to sense her. There was a deliberate cut-off... Lucifer had a rough idea where she had gone off to but there was something blocking him from getting close to Lilith. That's where he needed my help. I could sense that this being, whether it was THE Lucifer or not, was genuine in his pleas... in fact I got the sense he was worried I may harm him.

It was on that pretense I agreed.

The next thing I knew Lucifer paced his hand upon my forehead and we were transported somewhere dark. I seemed to... glow... the light of my being illuminating my surroundings. There were whispers, the drops of water echoing through elaborate cave systems. It seemed like we had somehow gone underground, but the state I was in made the space feel much more vast than I anticipated.

AI Depiction of Lucifer Pleading for Dakota's Help

I followed Lucifer down some steps, seeing vines gripping the walls, until we reach a large opening that Lucifer seemed warded from.

He couldn't pass through, no matter his efforts, but I was unhindered by the barrier.

I traverse further, finding an opening illuminated by a large flame. A river passed through, more vine-like plants growing into the surroundings, all leading to a large flat stone where a woman laid upon her side. It was Lilith, beaten and rattled by Cain. It took some convincing... the fact that ~~censored~~ saw me as a friend and the possession revealed Cain was afraid of me, it didn't take much for me to get through to Lilith. She apologized... the situation was just too much, assuring me she would return to ~~censored~~ in a couple days. That's when the vision Lucifer induced stopped...

The following morning, I received a text from ~~censored~~ confirming Lilith had in fact come back. According to ~~censored~~, Lucifer confirmed he had solicited my help.

Where did he take me though? Hell? Hades? Inner Earth? With all that has come forward I am reevaluating nearly everything.

February - March 2021

The following is a summary report of the events during and after the ~~censored~~ attacks:

Entity: ~~censored~~
AKA: Shadowman
Lord of Shadows
Death
Location: Global

Classification: Dangerous Intelligent Entity
Likely Nephilim
Potentially Godlike

WARNING:

This entity has shown the potential to cause significant harm or even death. Those who feel they may not be in the best state of mind should probably avoid reading this text in detail as it may make you a susceptible target. The Hat Man is highly intelligent, most likely older than nearly every religious practice known to man, and has proven itself to be capable of almost every alleged form of spiritual attack. Personal information involving various individuals will be mentioned in this report for simple documentation and reference purposes only. This information has been shared by the individuals in question and is NOT by any means meant to discriminate against any of them. For the safety of civilians outside of the company, and who haven't established a public appearance, names have been altered.

Summary:

First identified by author -censored- is an entity that visits countless people seemingly around times of personal trauma. Most eyewitnesses report he appears in times of poor mental health, domestic violence, and drug use. Often he is stated to appear in the bed of night in his intended target's bedroom and just watches. He has also been known to show up at locations of significant tragedy that may respond to the circumstances mentioned above. It seems most common that individuals report visitations from this entity right around puberty. -censored- has set up a point of contact on her official website to send in encounters with the entity or request her aid. She has also published two books regarding the entity, shadow people in general, and how to deal with them. Her publication company and herself have also trademarked the terms -censored- allegedly as an effort to throttle misinformation to prevent further injury to potential victims.

AI Depiction of "Lord of Shadows"

Personal Encounter:

I know not how long this entity has had its eye on me. The earliest I can account for something similar to its presence was roughly at the age of three. This was after my life was almost taken by my stepmother, but I could fight back. At the age of fourteen, I had learned my father was being charged for sexually assaulting one of my sisters; and it prompted another visit from this thing. Only this time, it spoke, offering me a deal to join him in return for the death of my father. As for what, I don't know. Other voices that came through pierced my own as I yelled for it to get away, and it seemed to deter it.

Other times when it appeared circumstances were surrounding further domestic violence, suicidal tendencies, violent and psychotic episodes, etc... For location reference - the incident involving the knife and my stepmother took place in November 1999. In 2001, I somehow transported 30 miles away from home. Thankfully the location I turned up was my grandparent's house, likely in response to possible trauma (psychic teleportation or alien abduction has been suggested). When I learned of the charges against my father and the subsequent deal, it was June of 2012.

Preliminary Research:

Outside of the book by -*censored*-, not much information was present to fully understand this entity or its motivations outside of the uneasy feelings numerous witnesses claimed to receive. As this was a continuing pattern, the official investigation, as "Specialist of the Strange" and other previous titles, was put on hold until further notice. The standard procedure was, and in many ways, guiding the clients into overcoming the traumas that may have triggered the Hat Man's appearances. Eventually, he will lose power and interest. With this veil of mystery, it seemed the entity was relatively harmless, just a figure that took joy in misfortunes enough to where he may influence it to come. Even mentions of this entity, and possibly connected phenomenon, are said to be lures for further troubles.

A Change:

For years I shelved the investigation into this entity as nothing new seemed to come forward. However, in a casual conversation with my ex, -*censored*- I was told of her encounter with the -*censored*-. Interestingly enough, it showed a deviation in behavior. When visiting a former boyfriend in the summer of 2015, she reported that something slammed a bathroom door on her and held it shut. This was right as a shadow apparition matching the description of the -censored- pulled out a knife and charged at her former significant other. Needless to say, the relationship didn't last much longer afterward. -censored- managed to fit all the criteria mentioned above for -censored- victimology for lack of a better term. She had apparent signs of childhood sexual assault and obvious strained relationships with her parents. Severely abused as a child to the point large chunks of memory were missing.

As is unfortunately common for most young ladies of that mindset, she frequented abusive relationships that may or may not have subconsciously reminded her of those times. She never worked up the courage to share the fullest extent of what has transpired with me, aside from feeling triggered at the sight of "kill room" scenes from the Showtime series "Dexter." The telling of this encounter stirred further interest in the phenomenon because any different deviations would provide better insight. Comparisons between -censored- other eyewitness accounts hint at very little change in modus operandi. However, another pattern tied directly to episodes of sleep paralysis draws even more curiosity.

This entailed a "tall, slim, shadow" standing above a witness either just before falling asleep or being jarred out of a deep sleep yet not fully conscious. It needs to be noted these visions do qualify as hypnagogia or hypnopompic (depending on whether the subject is falling asleep or is just waking up, respectively). For those unfamiliar with the terms hypnagogia or hypnopompic, these describe a hallucinogenic state of mind. These cause visuals from a dream-like state to still project visuals from a dream onto the waking world for the laymen. Those familiar with augmented reality may be more familiar with the concepts. As such states are often triggered by stress, the potential of this entity also making an appearance around the same time is not out of the question if not a complete hallucination of an overloaded brain

Outbreak:

The insanity of the COVID-19 pandemic, and 2020 as a whole, finally turned the tides of the investigation. I left a post on Reddit asking for stories relating to the ~~censored~~ A response from an anonymous user pointed me in the direction of Breton mythology to view versions of what most would be familiar as the "Grim Reaper" or otherwise a servant of Death itself. This version is known as the Ankou. As with most versions of mythologies across the globe, there are regional variations. The Ankou is sometimes described as a man or skeleton with a black robe and a large hat to conceal his face. Sometimes he may even just appear as a shadow apparition as well. One story that tries to explain the origins of the Ankou states that it is the last person, usually male, to die in the previous year. Another report says that there may be multiple Ankou at once, each one that stays within a specific region. Perhaps the most interesting of the tales is that the Ankou is none other than the firstborn son of Adam and Eve; Cain, aka the father of murder.

AI Depiction of Samael

In the light of this information, more research needed to be done on the events within the Garden of Eden that led to Cain becoming murderous. It was essential to not focus on a single religious text. Instead, analyze all accounts to get some idea of how the Hat Man may be connected if there was any potential to be a remnant from humanity's beginnings. Looking within Jewish lore, a piece of information about the serpent in the Garden of Eden was of interest. Most would think of the serpent in the Garden as none other than Lucifer. However, this is not the case, but quite possibly a case of mistaken identity. Lucifer is listed as a fallen angel, yes. No matter what religious text one should read, he is not the figure one may think of today in association with "Satan." Look through Hebrew translations of various texts, one would find that "Satan" was, in fact, used as a verb to denote an "opponent, adversary, etc..." Only when prefixed with "Ha," as in "Ha Satan," the word serves the purpose of a noun or title.

Going to early translations of Judeo-Christian texts, only one entity was ever called that directly. That being was named Samael, an archangel who ruled over Death itself and was speculated to be Cain's "biological father." After two weeks, a phone call came in on my hotline, right as I was returning home from work, that concerned a family out of North Carolina. Immediately, the overall vibe of the call just sang something sinister was going on. Whatever the matters at play, my moral obligations forced me to look deeper into the situation. The client mentioned whatever was attached to him seemed to be shifting its focus onto his three-year-old son. The conversation took roughly three hours to complete. Once enough time and effort were established to build trust with the client, he shared all the typical signs of demonic influences. Strange smells, deep scratches, things being thrown around, nearly all of the classic symptoms.

When the client, the family's father, was home alone, a particular entity matching the ~~censored~~ description would apparently sit down and talk with him about topics the father liked. When something would speak ill about the entity, objects would seem to be thrown towards people to warn them not to speak. There was also a particular room in the house, the wife called the "Dead Room," where it seemed just walking into it would cause one to become physically ill. As our chats continued, he admitted that there was one incident where this entity grabbed him by the neck in the middle of the street and slammed him into a nearby car. On the other end of the call, I could hear the gentleman walking through his house. As he walked to let the family dog outside, a secondary voice emerged, one that sounded like a small child.

The family consisted of a husband, wife, and one three-year-old child. The wife and child were already relocated to a town in Idaho. Upon asking the husband about the voice, he asked if it sounded like a five to seven-year-old. Apparently, the wife had suffered a miscarriage in that timeframe. It isn't unusual for miscarried children to pay their would-be parents a visit. The fact that the alleged child shouted the words, "If you don't hang up that phone now, you little bitch, I'll fucking kill you," was enough of a red flag to warrant further study. I asked the husband if, at any time during these conversations, did the entity identify itself. Obviously, the entity was trying to establish trust, so if you're going to be friends with someone, you obviously need to know each other's names. The name given was "Cain," and Cain was trying to recruit the husband with promises to be a "general" in his army (as the husband put it). I provided the family with a protection sigil I designed with the aid of the archangel Michael. It was initially crafted in response to a case out of Pittsburgh to help a family stalked by a corrupted soul of a child rapist and murderer. This case drew in UFO activity throughout its duration and even caught the attention of Ed and Lorraine Warren.

When writing this report, it is unknown if these facts are relevant outside of illustrating the magnitude of the case. The negative spirit was a man who likely raped and murdered two young girls known of. With the sigil administered, the activity was brought to an end for both these cases. As for the family from North Carolina, it should also be noted that the father admitted to me to experiment with the recreational use of DMT at a young age. DMT is a chemical that is believed by some to be connected to the spiritual phenomenon. The son had shown early "sensitivity" to paranormal elements, which may have been influenced by his father's DMT use (which occurred long before the child was born). Still, it is likely he will grow out of it in time.

A few days after the encounter with the family in North Carolina, a figure appeared in my bedroom that offered to reveal information helpful to the case. Its appearance was short, roughly five feet in height. Hiding within the veil of shadow it cast, I swore I could see the curves of a woman. The figure's eyes seemed to appear first from the cover, with a gentle and welcoming smile. I could make out more details of her appearance as she revealed herself. She looked of middle eastern descent, with sparkling brown eyes, olive-toned skin, and curly black hair. I asked her for her name, which her reply was, "I've had many names, but you know me as Eve." Eve approached me, placed her hand on my temple, and started to show me visions of what I could only assume was the Garden of Eden. I had a sense of familiarity as if I was there before. Eve proceeded to walk me through her affair with Samael. She showed how Adam mistreated her and Cain because of the ordeal, with Cain holding deep resentment and anger that grew with the abuse. Finally, she showed him snapping.

Abel was the typical annoying younger brother Adam favored and seemed to boast about being the "favorite" child. This was the moment that Cain was driven to murder his brother, leading to the famous curse. By Eve's hand, I was able to see the act take place. Abel managed to successfully land one good blow by slamming a rock into Cain's face. Upon realizing what was happened, Abel tried to beg for mercy, which only angered Cain more. This is likely the true origin of the "Mark of Cain." Sightings of one Hat Man figure's "true face" mention possible scar tissue on the right side of the face. A month later, a woman reaches out to me in regards to postings online. I made inquiring stories about the Hat Man and asked if I knew anything. Upon hearing that I had done an episode of my podcast dedicated to my findings until that point, she was adamant about listening to it before talking to me. She soon got back to me frightened, explaining that she was being visited by this thing around the time her 5-month-old son was born. She grew scared when the entity seemed to focus on the baby. However, she was even more nervous at the news of the Hat Man's real identity being Cain, as that was the name she gave to her child. She was administered the sigil to help ward off the child and has had no more encounters with the entity.

Enter "THE COMPANY":

I utilized my social media management service to frequently post a notice across my various pages. This was to start pulling together more stories to plot a potential documentary to further explore the phenomenon beyond the "he's just evil" narrative that is currently present. In collecting more stories, -censored- initiated a global effort to gather more information on the entity. During the begin-ning stages of this, an attempt was made to speak to -censored- directly. Unfortunately, her trademarking the term made any discussions beyond that nonexistent. Her reason-ing behind the move was to utilize legal methods to curb the spread of misinformation that could lead to further harm or death. However, her manner in speaking does hint that she is more about capitalizing on her "discovery." As this was the case, the investigation moved forward. Priority one was to establish a timeline of where and when this thing ap-peared and gather full testimonies from eyewitnesses. I had my doubts about this approach. It seemed heavily rooted in episodes involving severe trauma that often gets obscured as the mind attempts to protect itself. Still, it was the best thing to go on. Many started to simply copy and paste reports from posts on the social media page Reddit, some of which were taken from responses to my posts. This approach may seem simple enough to the novice but obviously proved, partially, the main flaw I was concerned about. Thanks to a sequence of attacks on February 12th and 13th during live streams on the *-censored-* YouTube Channel, these matters were soon forgotten.

As if conveniently planned, most of the damage took place on the 13th as the entity took out members on panel one by one, seemingly traveling thousands of miles in a matter of minutes. This led to one member, -censored- becoming possessed and promptly exorcized on-air; and the official termination of the investigation. In the weeks that followed, the team faced unusual amounts of mental trauma from within the company. One such member even has to take mental health leave due to personal circumstances, -censored-. Analysis of audio collected by myself during these attacks returned the messages, "Quit hunting us," "Tear him apart," and the names of two members explicitly named as targets. These members were -censored-.

Likely, multiple entities came through on those recordings, even ones who tried to help the team. One other member, -censored- who was in the focus of the attack, claimed she was left with babysitters designated by the -censored- Due to hostile behaviors from -censored-, it is unknown whether or not these reports are accurate. Unfortunately, the safest assumption in that regard would be to assume they were, in fact, false. Efforts are best allocated to help further assist other victims. One last portion that should be noted is another member who was not on the panel, -censored- was also attacked upon trying to perform Reiki protections. In comparison, the attack was minor, with symptoms akin to a light sunburn. She was quickly advised to walk away to protect herself and her young children.

In the Dark:

I had a gut feeling that Hat Man was not going to simply leave us be. This is something that could simply step to the left and view his victim's entire world, down to every movement of their internal organs and every little thought in their mind. Have it step right and it's thousands of miles away.

I took on the investigation further, gathering more reports of encounters, more concerning patterns arose. One involved a young man who swore vengeance against the entity for the deaths of his father and best friend. Another involved a mother concerned for her three year old daughter who frequently would shout, "Go away shadow man!" This would be just before she claimed something pushed her down the stairs. Another was a woman reported she had dealt with intense visitations from shadow people before Minimal contact was kept with -censored- to respect their need to heal. Still reeling from the experience, likely due to reminders of past trauma, -censored- had all records of the entity wiped from -censored- systems to prevent encouraging unprepared individuals from instigating another attack. I know not if this was coincidence or if by some psychic link, but after a couple weeks had past work was done to start severing the dark energies surrounding both -censored-. Occult energies were worked in response to severe the connections, first starting with -censored- as she claimed that the -censored- left behind other -censored- to watch her and the team. I attempted to make a deal with the -censored- which offered him a chance to spread his terror without having to lift a finger, in exchange for pulling away from -censored-.

This was to buy time then orchestrate a clever counter assault against the -censored- to render him powerless outside of potential duties as a version of the Grim Reaper. Within hours -censored- reached out to report the entities were gone. Apparently there was a conversation that took place between the entities that involved mention of "the Knowing One." After -censored- was made aware of the deal, she figured they were talking about me. I pondered an idea presented by -censored- to use occult practice to create some form of -censored- to combat any further attacks. Another sigil was designed to help create the being, later to be dubbed the "Knight of Light." The name was picked through poetic contrast to further the intent of it being a protective entity; binding energies from the archangel Michael to counter potential influence from the only being known as Satan. Within a couple weeks of circulating this image, the woman who's child was being stalked by a -censored- came forward and Knight of Light Sigil mentioned that her four-year-old daughter claimed she was saved by the "Knight Light." The curious bit, was that during a video call the little girl happened to see me on the other end and grew excited, screaming, "Momma, he's the Knight." No other incidents have been reported. Within the same week -censored- started to slowly recover from his treatments enough to make appearances more with the company. It has been noted on a few occasions that a shadow figure could be seen behind -censored-, watching him. This

I AM THE SPECIALIST OF THE STRANGE | 183

is speculated to be the same "watcher" that -censored- had experienced at her own place.

Months later while backstage for aftershow hangout after a taping of -censored- furthered that he had wanted to bring up the topic of angels for some odd reason and having been a fan of my previous works through the paranormal streaming network -censored- the discussion shifted into my first encounter with the little girl known as Olivia. Upon hearing this discussion, -censored- came forward about having dreams involving a strange little girl he never met before.

AI Depiction of Dakota and "Olivia" Charging into Battle

When he gave a rough description of what the little girl looked like, it triggered enough of a familiarity with me to investigate further.

How would I do this? Well, conveniently, I do have an uncle on my mother's side -censored- who physically looks like he could be my twin brother. Growing up, we were confused as one another all the time. -censored- has three kids, a boy and twin fraternal girls, who not only look like they could be my own but all had phases where they would call me Dad. I pulled out a baby picture of one of the twin girls, and -censored- was hysterical. The baby picture was nearly identical to the girl he saw, but he claimed his dream visitor was a few years older. I dug around for a picture that had myself and both of the girls, who were about age three at the time, and -censored- freaked out even more. The only other person who believed she had seen Olivia was -censored-, the previously held idea that my potential daughter was only visible to blood family was thrown out when -censored- came forward. The reason it wasn't with -censored- was because she and I found out we had similar genetic heritages so the possibility we were somehow distantly related was pondered but not yet proven. -censored- would also provide even more insight.

When the investigation into the Hat Man begun -censored- was the only member to come forward about having previous experience with the entity, which involved physical attacks that occurred with she was about fourteen years old. She also recalled nightmares where she was sitting in total darkness and would see the Hat Man's true face just staring at her from above. Other nightmares she believed were connected to the entity all shared a same general theme of being all alone in a time of crisis, possibly reflecting inner fears of not being "good enough" for healthy relationships. After the attack she had to take a leave of absence from -censored- in order to cope with mental health related issues. Out of respect I choose not to go too far into detail about what issues those were as they are not relevant to the situation at hand and to respect her privacy.

Interestingly enough I had a dream one night that mirrored the recurring nightmares ~~censored~~ had shared with me, the ones where she would be alone in the dark with the Hat Man staring at her from above. Only this time, I was able to intercept the dream, and approach the being from behind to attack it. The very next day, ~~censored~~ started communicating more with members of the team. When I got to talk to her ~~censored~~ and I discovered that not only were we close in age (her being born in December, 1995 and myself in January, 1996) but we had very similar profiles in astrology, psychic ability, and genetic heritage. We both even had attachments with strong entities, often viewed as polar opposites.

Further research through https://maps.leylines.ch/ helped discover that she and I would roughly the same distance from a minor ley line. These connections were speculated to render it possible for ~~censored~~ and I to send messages to one another via the Necrophonic app, and for Olivia to make appearances between the two of us. It was through ~~censored~~ I was able to get enough information to render an image of Olivia through apps similar used to age progress missing children photos. While recording episodes of their podcast they managed to capture the voice of a little girl saying "Ding dong" like she was trying to get their attention, as well as what sounded like a tired "Mommy." The second EVP captured ignited speculation that ~~censored~~ may have been her real mother, but it would soon turn out that theory didn't hold much water as information came forward that proposed the possibility Olivia was not traveling alone. -censored-'s image was also used to render the picture of Olivia, to which -censored- would later confirm to be an exact match.

Two possibilities come out from this information. The first being that Olivia was not alone, but was being guided by "mommy." Reports from individuals claiming to have sensitivities to paranormal energies came forward, stating that Olivia seemed to be holding someone's hand but the witness could not see a figure. The second possibility, which may still hold some merit is that -censored- had some physical resemblance to Olivia's real mother and Olivia herself may have vision problems. A connection between -censored- and myself would be further tested when -censored- an emergency message starting with "Call Dakota, I think I just saw Olivia."

AI Depiction of the Resuce

-censored- had mentioned that a little girl with blonde hair had been spotted around his place, since before meeting me, so it is a possibility that Olivia has been watching over certain people for quite some time on top of visiting me. The emergency message contained an SOS that detailed -censored- had seen Olivia moments before being attacked and potentially possessed by a shadow entity. When the possibility of possession was presented, ~~censored~~ and I began working on a remote exorcism to sever the connection from ~~censored~~. I had a Necrophonic running which helped monitor the situation. Olivia signaled when the connection to ~~censored~~ was severed and he would soon call ~~censored~~ and I. This is when we learned that ~~censored~~ was physically being compelled to avoid the phone at all costs, feeling the sensation that something was growing increasingly angry when he would think of calling me for help. The rendered image of Olivia was later shown to ~~censored~~, to which he confirmed with the distinction he didn't get a clear look at her face.

Daddy's Girl... from Outer Space?

To the best of my knowledge, Olivia first appeared in my life at the age of twelve. Though with recent events, she may have been around longer, though the possibility of time travel remaining leaves establishing a timeline nearly impossible. Olivia would appear at random whenever my mind would slip into a darker place, in order to offer words of encouragement. Three other incidents took place where Olivia would appear in order to warn me of a coming death, either to offer support or to warn me of coming danger. Rendering of "Olivia Hope" based on a total of 13 witnesses.

The second encounter came the day I lost my maternal grandfather, my mother's father, to cancer. She appeared and offered to let me use her sight to see my grandfather's dying moments via astral travel. I would have been in the room personally, but as the oldest sibling I was tasked with keeping the younger ones and dogs locked in a separate room to avoid them getting in the way of emergency personnel. Little did she and I both realize, my grandfather was in a condition that allowed him to see her in the room. The third took place in October of 2014. I was in a car accident, struck by a pickup truck going 60 mph.

The impact was hard enough for me to go unconscious. However, I believe without a doubt that Olivia appeared in the car just moments before impact, screaming "Daddy! Look out!" The third took place in April of 2016, while I was in Paris, France. My tour group was on a riverboat cruise to admire the lightshow of the Eiffel Tower when suddenly it started to rain. The group and others on the boat hid in the deck below to hide from the elements while I stayed topside. A tap on my shoulder initially gave me the impression that I was standing in the way of someone's photo. When I looked back to see who it was, I was shocked to see it was my grandfather standing side by side with Olivia. The two of them mentioned that they weren't going to be visiting as much as they were as I no longer needed their guidance as much. I can validate from EVP recordings of various cases my grandfather still checks in from time to time to see where my ventures take me.

This report would likely not be as long had Olivia stopped appearing. In time I came to realize that they both were just trying to help keep me going. As for why Olivia has become more active, that is still up to speculation. After joining ~~censored~~ I created two films for the streaming network ~~censored~~, one titled "The Hunt for Olivia," to explore more about what I knew involving the "Olivia Paradox" as I called it. The other was "Bonds of Beyond" designed to explore overlap between the ET/UFO phenomenon and Spirit Phenomenon. It should also be mentioned that there was an earlier experiment titled "The Hunt for Infinite Earths" that inspired Bonds of Beyond further.

All these projects brought out a number of names of entities that may be showing interest.

These entities are as follow:

- Michael the Archangel
- Gabriel the Archangel
- Metatron
- Yeshuah

    - Actual name of Jesus
    - Translates directly into the name Joshua
- Yahweh?
- El?
- Ashtar?
- Vrillon?
- Athena?
- ~~censored~~

    - Referred to as simply "John" in Bonds of Beyond
    - ~~censored~~

- Was based on real occult information
  - Several people involved in ~~censored~~ creation claim they saw and interacted him within our world
  - After a spirit box session was conducted, an audio message was left for Dakota with an unexplained source of white noise that said, "If you can hear me, ~~censored~~ wants you."
- Aleister Crowley

  - Spirit box communications were held to reach out to Crowley to see if he knew anything about the ~~censored~~
  - Has offered help in the fight
- By interacting with ~~censored~~ two more entities entered into focus

  - Lucifer
  - Lilith
- ~~censored~~ offered tips into more entities worth studying, believed to be connected to the Pleiadians.

  - Artemis/Diana
  - Apollo

UFO contact experiments were also conducted focusing on the members of the Ashtar Command, producing interesting video footage of strange objects appearing. When directing attention towards Ashtar's crew, Olivia would appear. It should also be mentioned that seemingly out of random I had a dream where I was taken to a futuristic hospital room where a woman laid in bed while holding a baby boy. Olivia was sitting next to the woman and upon realizing I was there, she looked at me and said, "Daddy, come meet my baby brother." When I woke up, the work "Tachyonis" came out of my mouth. A quick Google search revealed a theoretical particle, speculated to be involved in time travel, that was claimed by various new-age groups to be the source of the Pleiadians space travel capability. The next day, ~~censored~~ (psychic medium) mentioned to me that she needed to one day talk about my experience.

~~censored~~, who goes by the name ~~censored~~, also gave me a "mini-reading" through a Zoom call where Olivia's voice came through the speaker. All these interactions help render even more images of Olivia's potential mother, and a grown version of her baby brother.

INFORMATION OF INDIVIDUALS OMITTED FROM PUBLIC RECORD FOR PRIVACY

Project: Knightshade

With the added influence of extraterrestrials it seems that ~~censored~~ may be on the verge of something that will change the world, hopefully for the better. I know not if it is entirely true that my own matters are a catalyst for this series of events to evolve, but as anyone can see it would be dumb of me not to include it. I truly feel that we are being left a trail of breadcrumbs that will lead us to the ultimate truth about reality.

It is also said that the biggest rule of working with the Ashtar Command (or Galactic Federation) is that if they offer to help us, we CANNOT hold that information for selfish gain. If we work together, we might just push the efforts of our organizations to new heights. This report does not signal the end of the investigation. I myself have spent the better part of thirteen years trying to understand the situation with my daughter. However, it has been made crystal clear that this has been a part of me for much longer than that.

My family heritage has 400+ years of paranormal sensitives, psychics, witches, you name it (to the best of my knowledge that is). In the year 2020, right as these events with -censored- kicked up, my home state of Idaho had the highest number of reported UFO sightings in the US. I grew up in a haunted small town. The room I tried to take my own life in was the same room I ended up in after the possible alien abduction incident when I was six. It was also the same room my grandfather passed away in and saw Olivia for the first time.

I remember visions of the -censored- logo. There is too much here for it to all be coincidence. Moving forward, I suggest furthering the study into the Ashtar Command. As well as establishing more of a profile on the -censored- and possible ways to divert future attacks, just in case. Some of the patterns indicate that the to-be-dated Japan trip may have something more waiting for us, in already dangerous territories. I plan on researching more into occult methods to provide safety to members of ~~censored~~ and the public we release this information to. I believe the Japanese have an equivalent of voodoo dolls we may be able to use as a sort of stand-in should we get attacked. I highly suggest we keep certain personal details out for the protection and respect of everyone involved regardless of current standings or previous indiscretions. In the event of releasing this information to the public, we need to drip feed the masses to lure out any more potential leads that may be beneficial to the investigation.

Due to aforementioned trademark restrictions, we will need to call the ~~censored~~ by another name. I can suggest the name "Lord of Shadows," as I refer to him in my book "Dear Kota: Time to Fess up." Once we are ready, we can present our findings to the public. This can be an opportunity to further the company's focus into bettering mental health. Instead of portraying it like a horror documentary, my idea is something more like an Avenger's formatted presentation. All forms of people, on and off world, coming together to combat a common enemy and better the world as we go. This will also provide ways to cross market other ~~censored~~ related brands, and give participating members a chance to promote their own works. If this is going to work, we need everyone. Active members of ~~censored~~ listed in this document are to be given top priority in coming together.

Opportunities for others to participate will be available as well.

9
Extraterrestrial Revelations

March 2nd, 2021
"Martian Infirmary"

Seemingly a normal night, as the ~~censored~~ attacks seemed to be coming to an end, I was taken to what looked like a hospital room out of Star Trek, being led by a man with long brown hair who was roughly my height.. Metallic doors opened sideways, revealing a woman lying in a bed holding a newborn baby. Olivia was with the woman, hanging over her shoulder. Olivia realizes I'm in the room and says "Daddy, come meet my new baby brother." I walk over to the woman's side and smile at the newborn baby boy, who looked alot like me. The woman's image was somehow being blocked out like a hidden character in a video game.

As I was staring at the boy, giving my daughter a kiss, I looked to a wide window on my left and saw the landscape outside the facility looked like the Martian surface. Dumbfounded I asked if that was where we were and the man just chuckled, as if he knew I was going to make that remark, before starting to correct me. As he started to say the name of the location, an alarm sounded off and immediately the man grabbed my shoulder and said "we need to get you out of here now!"

AI Depiction of Iveena in "Martian Infirmary"

Obviously I was overwhelmed. I wanted to say and see the baby but I was also trying to figure out what the heck was going on. The next thing I knew, I was physically flying into my bedroom through the wall like something out of Peter Pan. I hovered briefly over my bed before feeling something yanked me downward with enough force that the metal frame of the bed snapped in multiple places and even went through the wall.

October 28, 2021

Earth - United States - Idaho - Between Filer and Curry - Just off Highway 30

Driving home from a Halloween/Birthday party, a bright orange craft octagonal in shape suddenly appears about 10 feet in the air just off the side of the road. The craft seemed no more than 15-20 feet in diameter and had a wobble. Brief glimpses in the window showed grey-like beings, who seemed equally as surprised to see me as I was of them. The ship disappeared before I had a chance to stop the car and try to get a photo.

AI Depiction of Airk Ship

Likely species of grey are listed as Airk, essentially intergalactic geologists. Idaho, being known as the "Gem State," has several locations where one can mine for crystals. The Airk usually don't interact with people, mostly just use Earth as a quick pit stop before taking off somewhere else.

Some have asked me if there was any "bad feeling," about this encounter, possibly due to prejudice towards those who fit the "Grey" description. But, no, just mostly surprise. Those beings seemed just as surprised to see me as I was of them.

February 2022

I was notified of an individual in the UK allegedly suffering from multiple, multiple medical ailments thanks to a generational curse instilled by the goddess Kali. The story told to me that the gentleman, riddled with ailments so severe he was attached to a colostomy bag, had been sexually assaulted by some form of Succubus; and that his predicament was the result of a curse laid on his family. Apparently his grandfather had committed atrocities during bouts of religious violence between the Hindus and Muslims in India; one particular young lady that was sexually assaulted by him had a father-figure who was burned alive that may have been a sahir.

So, to put it in layman's terms, I was dealing with a young man who was so damaged by a vengeful father figure...

It became obvious that something nasty was tied to the young man. Stories of literal garbage shoved into the woman's throat likely was the source of the abdominal disruptions, and the succubus... immediately that rang like revenge. It wouldn't be the first time I've come across an entity who got people mixed up, if it was a generational curse something as little as having a strong family resemblance could be enough for the "curse" to transfer.

Unfortunately I had to pass this on to someone more local to the client, but not after I made at least one attempt to speak directly to the entity in question. I researched Kali, organized a bit of a channeling/summoning using a combination of my protection methods and a psychic jumpstart (soaking my feet in salt water) to put myself in a deep enough trance to approach the client and address the being on it's own turf.

AI Depiction of Psychic Confrontation

When I made contact, the succubus was clearly, trying to dig itself further into the client's physicality to afflict more damage. Centered in it's haze was the client, almost giddy at the attention. It became clear something else was motivating this curse. The visuals which overcame me are hard to describe, like two gods bending reality on a whim to try outdoing one another, but seeing I was not so easily swayed I managed to earn enough respect for the bring to take me back to when the affliction started.

Through the victim's eyes, I watched the soliders burn her "father" alive, the father's spirit crying out in anger and swearing vengeance as she was violated. The anger I felt within... I knew all too well. There was not even a need for English, I understood everything perfectly. Then the vision moved forward in time to more modern day... showing the client starting to take advantage of a young lady.

I managed to convince the entity to break it's connection, seeing the man trying to harm another reignited old angers, but that notion was tearing away at the very soul and corrupting their being. Did they really desire their afterlife to be torn by vengeance? Giving into those emotions, at least in theory, made many literal demons... they had to let go. But the damage done was likely irrepairable. If this being was telling the truth about what the client was doing, I wouldn't necessarily have a problem leaving him to rot... but even I know that trying to seek revenge on those who do us wrong usually amounts to nothing more then skinning yourself just to have something to hit others with.

There was one condition I had to follow to break the entity's influence, to walk away as well, which under the circumstances I agreed and left the reasoning to the fact I did not have necessary funds to personally head to the UK for proper investigation and having the client pay for my plane ticket was wrong. Some rather shady individuals tried to lay claim to the case, as for what happened with them I do not know. My sources on the other side say that the being was lifted to someplace else for them to be allowed to heal, which was a relief in itself because the communication ritual I did to make the ordeal left me physically weak and hardly able to get out of bed for about three days.

April 16, 2022

Interview with ~~censored~~ on Bald and Bonkers Show, information about various ET species mentioned in this text and her advice guides my search for answers to new heights. I managed to ask her a question, as several indications hinted that I had a wife in a separate life, if any relationships I was in down here were considered as cheating. The reaction, obviously while unexpected, sparked quite a bit of laughter. But ~~censored~~ suggested that if someone involved in a starseed program had a romantic partner, that their partner's in this life would likely subconsciously remind them of their other life. This sparked an idea.

"Older" Rendering of Iveena

Being that I had Olivia's picture, what if I used AI to essentially weed out my features to create a possible photo of her mother? I utilized a feature on a phone app called FaceApp (a feature now since deleted) to take Olivia's picture and used photos online of various celebrities I had crushes on throughout my life to enhance certain features.

Eventually, when I reached a certain point in the creation process, my heart sank and I started to becoming emotional. I ran outside, crying to the stars begging for forgiveness because... upon seeing her face... certain memories started to surface. The feelings behind them, most confusing of all, were ones where I felt like I somehow failed her. I felt like I wasn't the man she and the kids deserved to have in their life, literally falling to my knees underneath the stars. In a moment of silence, I saw a flash of light moving through the sky that felt like someone was trying to get my attention. The light directed my attention to the Pleiades. Whether this was intentional or not, I don't know, but what stood out the most was the voice I heard that was responding to my cries...

"It's okay Dakota, we hear you, we know."

April 24, 2022

Earth - United States

While recording a live show, a guest expressed interest in CE5, contact, and various other topics. Her real name was revealed on air through a spirit box session. After recording she reveals a screen memory she believed was covering an abduction. She remembered seeing herself as a young girl in a Christmas themed nightgown, being taken out of her house, and seeing a "bucking moose."

Summer 2022

Iron City Paranormal captures strange anomaly involving SLS camera and a computer they had me sitting on through video call. Either they caught y projection coming out of my computer or something physically manipulating the wifi signal to talk to me. They invited me on through a video call to a case to see if I would get any psychic feels of the old tattoo parlor, and to make this entry short anytime I got an inclination of something going on, they captured some form of anomaly.

August 11th, 2022
Earth - United States - Idaho - Twin Falls

I was staying at a family friend's home while waiting for the new house to be ready to move into. My car was in the shop, so I would just walk to her place from work, which was barely over a mile. Thankfully the weather was nice most nights. I worked nights so I didn't have to deal with high temps too much.

One night, it was a fairly clear night, I decided to play Dr. Steven Greer's CE5 tones while walking. With the application, I found that if you messed with the pages in the app a certain way, the tones wouldn't stop playing and allowed you to play at least two separate recordings at once. This allowed for a bit of experimentation that might take a bit of leg work to replicate since recent updates fixed this loophole.

AI Depiction of Black Diamond UFO Flying Over Dakota

I played the recording labeled "crop circle tones," frequencies heard by electronic recording devices while documenting likely ET crop circle formations. I paired it with the tone labeled "Fibonacci sequence," a sound rendering with the Fibonacci mathematical sequence embedded into it. The main idea behind the CE5 protocols was to allow humans to go around government officials and establish contact with ETs. Different tones presented on the app would likely yield different sorts of manifestations to take place. My idea was to use the"standard" tone and pair it with the Fibonacci sequence, which was noted to help more subtle energy forms manifest easier.

The sound was directed through earbuds so only I could hear it. This was in part a cover for me so in the event someone panicked about seeing a 6'7" stranger walking around at night and called me into the police, I was just a guy walking home and listening to music. The other purpose helped direct the sound into my system so I could feel the electromagnetic charges that often took place in my head that seemed to flow in sync with the CE5 tones.

15 minutes into my walk, roughly the amount of time the app notes it should take for something to manifest, a dark grey diamond craft appeared right above me. I had other instances of possible craft in the distance that seemed to respond to the tones, but they were far enough to appear as specks of light.

When I first noticed it, I genuinely thought that maybe a large owl was flying off of the 40 ft tree I was next to. The ship then flew directly into the light of the full moon, casting a faint shadow. The diamond was close enough for me to clearly make out the seamless design of the metal, the lack of any sort of lights, etc… it was close enough to where had I been quicker to pull out my phone, I would have caught a damn good picture. By the time I was able to do so, the craft took off. I would estimate that it was flying a good 100 -150 feet off the ground.

September 27th 2022

A quick journal entry

Wide area seemed shiny.. Short being, pale greenish skin, large oval eyes, saw me arrive as I changed out of my clothes into a uniform. Didn't react. Uniform was metallic grey, blue stripe down the torso. Hurriedly got dressed, seeking out someone. Found a seemingly familiar face. Elradon? Tall, darker skin, wider eyes, somewhat more pronounced skull. I asked if my wife or kids were near, he said he hadn't seen them. Must be on assignment. Found a note addressed to me, a woman's handwriting. Another clue? The only word I remember is Enoch...

October 2nd, 2022

A quick journal entry - Recall Dream

I was on Earth, mostly. Suburban neighborhood. Indiana? I remember seeing the Great Lakes as we were rushing down in a small craft.. Possibly late 80s, early 90s based on vehicles nearby. Two figures took a child, a young girl wearing a bright red Christmas themed dressed. One of the things, likely Greys, ran a long finger over her body. It didn't seem to notice me hiding in their craft. As I ambushed them, I discovered more children. More men, GFW, assisted in recovery and wiped the kids' so they wouldn't remember.

As we got back to the main ship I remember staring out a wide window looking at the Earth. Another man approached me to check on me, apparently this was to be my last mission for a bit. The other man, tall, very chiseled facial features... Ahel Pleiadian? I asked him if he thought the kids would be okay to which he assured me, asking about my thoughts on my upcoming envoy deployment. I made a remark about wondering if I would ever see those kids down there, and if I would remember. The other man smiled, winked, and said something along the lines of "Don't worry, you will. Just remember the moose." The man then held up three fingers in a triangle formation and pressed them up to my forehead. I jerked back and asked what he was doing, to which he said "You know the protocol, you're about to leave and we need to make sure you and the children are safe."

A took a deep breath and caved. Upon waking up, I realized who the child was and who the Pleiadian was...

October 4th, 2022

A quick journal entry - Recall Message

The following played in my head during a recall meditation, like it was some kind of voicemail.

You are Alerayon Teuitre of oraa nataru Shari. You and your family are involved with hybridization and giving aid via the Envoy program. You selected a vessel primed with Taali blood to allow yourself to tap into psychic potentials for when you encountered darkness. The one you know as archangel Michael is of this bloodline as well. But things aren't quite as you understand.

I don't know if I heard it correctly, or even spelt the names right... after further analysis I asked ~~censored~~ if she knew of a being by that matched the description of the one I saw and if he, at some point, worked with her contact. She confirmed that there

AI Rendering of Elaryon

was in fact a gentleman matching the same description I gave, to which I revealed may have been me. It was also somewhat of a shock to read that she and I have actually met before I came to Earth for this envoy mission. Which would explain why I felt so compelled to seek her out, she was a genuine thread to who I really was.

As for the connection to Michael the archangel, that is a connection I need to establish further. The connection was first suggested by priests I first consulted in regards to Olivia's first appearances. However further incidents, mainly revolving around the Hat Man / Cain, indicated a much more personal involvement.

One of the witnesses I put together a profile on disclosed to me an incident which Cain (or someone he controls) attacked him in a library and a mysterious stranger with a powerful, angelic vibe came to the rescue. There was a bright flash of light and both disappeared. The only marker of that incident left was a first degree burn on the man's hand of the letter M. Given the situation, the witness came to the conclusion his mysterious rescuer may have been archangel Michael. The weirdest part? The witness alleged that that Michael and I looked remarkably alike, almost as if we were blood relatives.

October 9th, 2022

Earth - United States - Idaho → Moonbase?

I was taken up in a small vessel. My children, my wife, and a fourth being were all present. We took a trip to living quarters on the moon (possibly) to simply have time to ourselves and discuss the future. Now that I learned the name of my Pleiadian vessel, that will open me to even more. It also seems one of last children I helped rescue is confirmed to be someone I met and had as a guest on the Bald and Bonkers Show. The Ahel Pleiadian, was ~~censored~~. ~~censored~~ confirmed all of this...

October 11th 2022

Earth - United States - Idaho

A quick journal entry

The young girl from previous entries, the one ~~censored~~ and I (along with others) managed to rescue, has been informed of the revelation. I scheduled a video call to tell her due to the significance of the information, clearly hitting on something she was trying to find out for years but had no luck. She was practically crawling through the screen as I told her. Other possible rescued kids may be coming forward as well but no confirmation.

October 22nd 2022

Earth - United States - Idaho

A quick journal entry

AI Depiction of Flying Pyramid

There's much chatter through the ethereal lines. I suspect in part that it may have something to do with the GSIC conference in Orlando. There was also a giant pyramid in the sky I saw outside my house while heading out for work. Or at least at first glance it looked liked a glowing white pyramid but it feels like there were more dimensions to it. It lasted for barely half a second. Possible Merkabah? It is a known kind of craft that certain species of ET are known to use... psychic projection based. I'll have to monitor...

November 6th 2022

Earth - United States - Idaho - Jerome

While I was recording a live, my mother sends me a text message saying "I know this might sound stupid but I thought I just saw a stationary green object in the sky near work." My mother is a 911 dispatcher for four counties, her work is stationed in ~~censored~~. When she has time, she often stops at either the nearby Ridley's, Walmart, or Dollar Tree to pick up last minute snacks to help her get through the night shift.

It should be interesting to note that I had a telepathic communication roughly two-three days earlier with my star family. It is said that if one has these kinds of connections, they may possess the ability to freely communicate on top of sharing psychic ability.

As I was driving on my way to work, I reached out and got a response from my son. The exact message I left was, "If you guys have time, and it is safe for you to do so, can you say Hi to your grandma?" My son simply said with a smile, "Sure thing, Dad, I get it."

AI Rendering of Michael

It's one thing for me to say that there was an immediate response. My wife and kids knew that while I accepted them with open arms, I was still trying to work on processing the entire situation. The thought was to try an experiment to see if my kids would be willing to show themselves to a neutral party, someone who had very little idea about the situation, but knew just enough to where they would contact me right away the second something happened. However, it still needed to be someone that my kids would have an emotional connection to (someone they would personally want to meet). What kid wouldn't want to go see Grandma and Grandpa?

November 24th, 2022

Iveena seems to have been visiting ~~censored~~ to help with their progress. We managed to positively identify her through the AI generated images of her and the kids; personally validating the visions I've been seeing. It would seem her and the kids share Intel about their visitations to others in the anticipation they would reach out to me for validation. The level of detail in the vision gets difficult in determining whether or not I'm physically there, I suppose that is to be expected. However a slight remark from ~~censored~~ about Iveena's and I sexual habits ended up being validated in the process. I have another child on the way, another baby girl. Iveena was wanting to wait until Christmas to reveal it but we took a few moments to talk over some names. Ireena...

AI Rendering of Ireena

I can't even share the news with everyone. One of my best friends is still skeptical about my ET origins, another is almost without a doubt compromised. ~~censored~~ are opening up to it... but it is still lacking. The very people I am sharing Thanksgiving with feel empty, seeing me as nothing more than an overgrown trash hound.

I want my family. It's been brought to my attention that there is apparently a way for me to leave, to be with them, but allegedly Galactic Law will forbid me from coming back until Earth is ready for interplanetary integration. Our job is to build the bridge for Terrans to join the Federation, and it seems that will start in two years.

So does that mean I will be gone? Can't say that I wouldn't say no...

Iveena, Olivia, Michael, and now Ireena...

If this keeps moving forward like it seems... I will be one lucky man.

November 26th, 2022

Last night my potentially compromised co-star of the main talk show in the company started going in on one of his alleged contact sessions. Just enough of a "weird" factor keys in to avoid me completely throttling him for his pride, however the more he opens his mouth the more I learn; something he seems to not yet grasp.

Should a soothsayer speak with ego, then that soothsayer is to be ignored, for their ego will forever blind them of what truths they may actually see. Especially one who dodges and misdirects the second he is confronted.

December 12th 2022:

-*censored*- left my company, proving likely a compromise from Grays. The people she was associating with openly promoted Gray interference. She also took issue with my handling of a couple incidents which she was involved with. Primarily that "I didn't take her side."

The first is when I addressed a fight that took place on a livestream. -*censored*- was apparently talking about how I was seen casting out Cain during the Valentines Day incident as well as how I managed to create a healing sigil that could combat strong negative influences. Someone on the panel -*censored*- was asking about the validity of the claims.

He was very professional about it, He felt that the way I was being painted made it sound like I "was going toe to toe with Thor (from the Avengers) in the streets of New York." Immediately -censored- took offense and started firing off. Everything got heated, and immediately people started blowing up my phone trying to paint -censored- in a bad light. I didn't respond right away because I was trying to get some sleep before I had to go to work.

I managed to convince the drama queens to give me a timestamp, so I could see what happened and not have to waste time trying to find it while I was getting ready for work. -censored- was asking an honest question. He wasn't being snarky or anything, he was just trying to acknowledge that my story is a bit more unusual than most. He even made a valid point that such blind devotion was a dangerous game to play.

The second incident involved claims of racial slurs. -censored- was broadcasting her grievances over a livestream due to someone calling her a "white girl." I watched through just enough of the stream to figure out who she was pissed at and reached out to get his side of the story without talking to -censored-. This just pissed her off. As she left the company, she just tried painting the situation as her slowly being squeezed out and took offense to me not begging her to stay.

Everyone, except myself, was legally considered a freelancer. They were able to come and go as they pleased. This was all signed in paperwork to protect everyone's interests.

I made sure to make it known her behavior was unacceptable, that everything was arrange for people to come and go as they please, and her ego was not wanted.

A third incident involving -censored- and the gentleman she was trying to scream racism at, his name was -censored-. On another stream, something seemed to be affecting -censored- to where he was hunched over in pain.

To me, it looked like he was having issues with his appendix.

To -censored- and the other so-called witches, he was possessed and they all started bustling out crucifixes. This ignorance pissed me off.

I played the protection sigil tone, slowly increasing the volume. The witches grew silent and tense, as if something was hunting them and they were curled in a corner, but -censored- responded. I increased the volume and -censored- seemed to no longer be in pain, only responding to my voice. I guided him back towards the surface without incident. Later that night though, there was an interesting turn of events.

AI Depiction of the Black Goo Being Extracted

I remember walking into a dark room, with -censored- laying naked on what looked like an operating table. I was suited up in a silver uniform, accompanied by my wife and two oldest. I was performing some kind of examination and remembered seeing some kind of black goo inside -censored- located right about his hips and was able to extract it without incident. However I noticed some irritation in the region that I was not able to directly operate on. It was like I was only authorized to clear the black goo and stabilize -censored- condition to a safe enough level that Earth doctors could handle it.

As we were getting ready to help -censored- get dressed, my wife pointed out I should make a mental note of a birthmark -censored- had. I asked her why, to which she explained "You're going to remember this so you can warn him to get to the doctor, you'll probably need something to prove that you did actually examine him."

I made a joke about her not pointing this out sooner. She just shook her head and said that I should listen better because she did tell me, pointing out the incident where I had a vision of an ex-girlfriend cheating and I spotted a tattoo on the guy to help validate what I saw.

We took -censored- home first before my wife dropped me off. Immediately the next morning I woke up to a group message with -censored- and a couple of the other "witches" talking to -censored-, vaguely dancing around the incident. In the chat I told -censored- point for point what happened the previous night and that it would be a very good idea that he get to the hospital soon to get checked out. I even pointed out where I saw a birthmark to solidify my point. -censored- became excited by the information I gave, saying that it was like I was reading his medical chart word for word.

Two days later, -censored- ends up in the emergency room with a ruptured hernia, exactly where I told him. While in the hospital, -censored- apparently had a doctor who looked like someone had superimposed my face to their body.

As that situation settled, I got to thinking about what my wife said to me about looking for identifying markers. It was then I realized -censored- was not the first person I took. The other from the Cain attacks were also taken by myself and my "colleagues." In some cases, I was just a familiar face to comfort the patient. Others I took a more active role. There were also incidents with these same people where I would make a remark about things I would have only known about if I was intimately familiar with them, or at least went on a beach trip with.

February 11th-12th 2023

On February 11th I invited -censored- on the show to talk about her book -censored- and the latest about UFOs being that the "tictacs" were a topic of discussion among the masses. During the show, there was the usual expected interference. I wanted to ask about the potential for more direct energy weapon attacks after I had a dream. Something about the dream itself seemed too detailed to just be a random visual.

I recall being in a city where beams of light were setting things ablaze. I look up and see a massive ship where the beams seemed to originate before almost being struck by one. For some reason the impression I got was that this dream was taking place in Texas, somewhere I've only been while on a layover at Dallas/Fort Worth.

I asked about the potential of future energy weapon attacks to -censored-, holding back any specifics to see what she might have. All she had to say on the matter was that the attacks were likely. The next morning, I find out my 16 year old cousin, -censored- and our grandmother were in a rollover crash. The vehicle rolled six times, almost ejecting my grandmother even though she was belted in. Grandma took the worst of it, which was especially unsettling as she was a heart attack patient. However -censored-

and my grandma both survived and have fully healed of their injuries.

February - March 2023

I was taken aboard a ship where the rest of my family was waiting inside, somewhat nervous for what was to come. It wasn't necessarily a negative vibe... more just anticipation. For what exactly? As it turned out we were on our way to a family reunion near Sirius B where my wife is from. The sector was liberated from negative influence involving the Greys, and GFW members were being allowed leave to visit families the left behind.

AI Depiction of Family Trip to Sirius B

The reason for the anticipation, the anxiety, was the fact that Iveena didn't exactly leave on good terms, something that she and I bonded over when I left Taalihara. But this time was different. Naturally she wanted to reconnect with her family, to simply just have the option to see them, even though her mother in particular and her had a bit of a strained relationship at times. But this visit had something more important behind it, Olivia and Michael had not yet met their grandparents in person. Iveena had also not told her parents about baby Ireena just yet, hoping to leave it as a surprise.

When we arrived I remembered being mesmerized by the crystalline structures. The feel in the air was like something out of old Sailor Moon manga, depictions of "Crystal Tokyo" as it was shown. Crystal, metal, nature... all working in unison to create a futuristic paradise. The sound of the metal echoing under our feel, the constant twilight sky thanks to the weak sun in the star system, this was to intense to be some... dream or hallucination. When we started to approach a certain building, there was an air of excitement and nervousness. It was time.

A man and a woman came out to greet us in front of their home. Both were roughly six feet in height, human looking. The ecstatic smiles upon the faces of everyone around revealed enough about who these people were. The woman looked much like Iveena, big green anime sort of eyes, smaller in frame from her age but in immaculate health. She had this way to just project her emotions towards others, as many from her world could do. The women there were also known to be quite physically expressive and known for their sexual ability. Iveena's father was a taller man, somewhat rounded features with graying dirty blonde hair. He didn't fit the almost anime-like appearance of others on this world, I believe he was originally an Ahel. When he approached me for a hug, it was like I was greeting an old friend.

The love, the joy, the happiness, the excitement quickly overflowed my senses. It was extraordinary to just feel such a connection with these people. Inside there were others awaiting, family friends on Iveena's side looking to reunited. Iveena's mother knew that I was coming for Earth, and set a holographic projection on the room we were in to almost resemble a holiday cabin. Machines scanned our DNA sequences to prepare a sort of gelatinous food that tasted magnificent. A part of me was not wanting to leave the festivities.

It was during polite chitchat Iveena's mother blurted something seemingly random that threw off the vibes for the evening. She seemed to be the type that had a tendency to blurt out whatever was on her mind, not giving much consideration to how it might affect others. She had asked me how my father was.

Naturally I was confused. I was still early in figuring out how to recall these events and the "father" I thought she was asking about now sits in an Arizona prison. I could almost hear Iveena trying to signal her mother to not push the question even further, trying to tell her that I didn't remember much. This only prompted further questioning on my part, to which Iveena let out a big sigh and set down the food she was holding, muttering how "it was only a matter of time..."

It was not the father I had on Earth, thank god, but my father from Taalihara. Iveena explained that my father had been on Earth to make up for the time lost after he urged me to leave home, feeling like he had somehow abandoned me when I needed family the most. He himself had taken on a envoy, not one of the same program I was in necessarily but enough of the genetic programming was in the family line to make this arrangement possible. Iveena had me focus deep into her eyes, placing her fingers against my temple, something she had done a million times before to help me relax.

"Think, Dakota. You already figured out that people can sometimes look and act similar to their other incarnations. You're father is not ~~censored~~, you really shouldn't be dealing with him but that's your choice at the end of the day. Think back to the day you left Taalihara, when your father told you to leave, who did he remind you of?"

For a few weeks before this trip, my so-called friend and brother in arms had tried to convince me that he was somehow my father from my ET left incarnated, trying to twist me away from those who tried to offer help. I played into the delusion, hoping it was just a simple matter that he's getting things twisted, but this slip of the tongue was more than enough for me to be able to truly address it.

After all, these beings saved my life. They're my family. They've been there for me through thick and thin, and aside from having doubts because of the extraordinary circumstances... I've never doubted their intentions. -censored- was giving a million reasons that multiple people have come forward wanting to address.

So.. who was my father? Only one man I knew on Earth fit all the criteria... my grandfather, who raised me like I was his own.

The second the realization hit me, more memories started to come back. Answers to questions I had about the seemingly spiritual connection my grandfather and I had from early age.

April 2023

Earth - United States - Idaho

My younger sister -censored- has confirmed with her doctor that she is in the early stage of pregnancy.

May 13th I had a visit from a young girl who strongly resembles -censored-. We talked about her older brother, who miscarried, and how that was how she knew that she could talk to me. She was worried about her parents, especially her mom, because the consequences of -censored- actions were upsetting her. The girl also revealed her name to be -censored-, she would be born just under 10 pounds, and that she would likely be born before her expected due date of December 5th.

Late April - May 2023 estimated

Federation Missions - Deployment

These last few weeks I have had on and off visits, all seemingly tied to Federation assignments. I remember feelings of pure adrenaline burnout, as if I was on the move. A trick that I've stuck with in order to tell if the certain visits upstairs were recent, or in my "other life" were whether or not I had hair.

AI Depiction of Dakota and Elaryon Showcasing the Similar Appearances

If I was bald, then I was acting as Dakota.

If I had hair, I was Elaryon.

For this one, I had hair.

It was a group deployment. Stealth was critical. As a way to suppress intel from Earth, those of us also tied to the envoy program would be given special attention to ensure the blocks in Earth vessels are effective to ensure as little combat detail makes it to the Terran population.

Funny how this ties into right about the time I meet -censored-. It should also be noted that about a week after meeting -censored-, my sister was the subject of a potential domestic terrorism accusation after someone used a fake phone number to pretend to be her and sent threats to her boss to shoot up the place. She was working at an assisted living facility for special needs adults. Needless to say she ended up losing her job.

In the interest of full disclosure, my sister hasn't exactly been making the best choices in who she associates with and this could purely be a bad-timing incident. Her formmer boss is known for starting fightings and lying to police, likely manipulated a mentally challenged baby daddy into pulling all this crap...

But within 24 hours after the last time -censored- was a guest on my show, and I discussed about potential approaching direct energy weapon attacks, my grandmother and 16-year-old cousin -censored- ended up in a nasty rollover that partially ejected my grandma even though she had on a seatbelt. Best to monitor how much I reveal in certain channels. It seems certain methods have been compromised. Either that... or my history of bad timing continues to this day.

May 4th, 2023

Location Unknown - Federation Deployment

Large corridor, I was in a squad of five. The other four, humanoid beings. In my arms was this large grey thing with weak tentacles drifting to the sides. It looked like a smaller version of the invaders from the Independence Day movies. Possible Negamuk? Not sure. It should be noted I had hair in this vision.

Negamuk said to be joining the GFW soon... was this a glimpse into the future? Or was I seeing things through someone else's eyes? I could feel everything in that moment, there was no way that could've been some intense dream... right?

May 27th, 2023

Earth - United States - Idaho

There was another visitation. This has been kind of repetitive. Where I was taken seemed dark, barely enough light was present to tell where something was in the room. The room I was in appeared almost Hollywood exaggerated tall, walls covered in what looked like Egyptian hieroglyphs, and there was a throne made to accommodate someone with a giant's frame.

As I jot this down, this may have been the throne room where I first met that being after the incident with my stepmom... the throne was empty and looked like it had been for some time. It should be noted near this time that a prominent figure, whose description closely matches who I saw, was taken into custody and the tides of the war starside were turning in the Federation's favor. Enlil... was it you? Had I taken your deal... who would I be now?

May 31st, 2023

Earth - United States - Idaho

Possible Intel/Recall

Surgical room. Dimly lit. Strapped to a table. I was weakened, being tortured. My chest was cut open as this thing reached its hand inside. I could feel everything, but started to disassociate from everything. The being looked human, but the eyes seemed to shift to reptilian. He taunted me, pressing a finger into my blood then rubbing it against my mouth. High pitched squeals came from the being's mouth, like it was trying to say something.. An explosion went off in another room, the being and others with it ran. I remember seeing a tall blonde man see me dismembered, pausing in shock for a brief moment before running towards me. Once I could the man was a friendly, I rested my head on the table I was stuck to and that was the end of the vision.

June 1st, 2023

Earth - United States - Idaho

Possible Intel/Recall

Futuristic city. I was at an event, looked like some kind of concert with friends. I was with a woman, alongside another couple. The woman resembled my wife, but a bit younger, almost teenage to early 20s. The other couple was darker in skin. The male, who resembled the guard from the earlier mentioned "Martian Infirmary" incident, felt like he was a best friend. He was tall, dark skinned, deep voice...

The event was wrapping up and myself and this other being got called to a medical office to aid pregnant women experiencing complications. We conducted thorough examinations and quickly were able to help the women, saving the babies, all seemingly as easy as putting a bandage on a papercut. The medical bay was able to show what the father looked like, resembling a humanoid iguana... the complications from the pregnancy itself seemed to be caused by incompatible DNA match... similar to known cases of RH incompatibility.

My colleague and I focused our attentions to separate women, exchanging information as we went along with the procedures. The medical bays could handle everything, we were pretty much there as emotional support as long as the machines didn't fail. If they did it would be on us to take the information given by the medical bays before the malfunction in order to administer the right treatments and prevent further harm.

June 4th, 2023

Location Unknown - Memory Recall

Dark area. The feeling in the air felt like a military base. I remember seeing the flash of a tall being. Slender... female... very high in command. I was with several other soldiers, all lined in formation. I don't recall seeing this woman before... but we were about to go into something hot and heavy. Casualties were expected.

July 3rd, 2023

Earth -> United States -> Arizona - Idaho

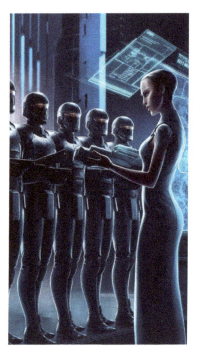

AI Depiction of Soldiers in Formation

First interview for Civilian Disclosure Project. Subject is -censored- who shows evident signs of a trauma-based psychic awakening. Likely abducted for SSP related activities at a young age. She revealed an attempt at taking her own life as being the likely cause of her awareness to her situation. I have been talking with her on and off personally as she wanted to reach out and get my perspective being that she and I are roughly in the same age group. Interview went well, I identified where her mental blocks were kicking in, indicating a fear of saying too much. Within 12 hours, I received a message from -censored- asking if I would hold off on releasing the interview. I should have expected this, but will politely respect her wishes. It should be noted she started to act distant after seeing the protection sigil. Only time will tell.

July 8th, 2023

I had an interview with -censored- for the Bald and Bonkers Show which had some noted interference and faint voices in the recording, as if someone was trying to hack into the frequencies. The interview was live so others heard it. It is extremely likely the voices were of my wife and -censored-. Some controversy stirred in the weeks that followed, connected to -censored-... the situation was serious enough that a voice came through while I was at work telling me to get home ASAP.

The controversy had spread to -censored- and fears of me being compromised due to... misunderstood information were expressed. I took to the airwaves to address the cowards too obsessed with drama to call them out, taking responsibility for my actions, and thanking -censored- who actually addressed her concerns with me directly. I wanted to lash out more... but I had other matters much more important. I was more pissed at the fact someone would dare to remotely insinuate I would do anything to harm someone who helped me understand my situation and find my family. I owe that woman an immense debt of gratitude and it stands against everything I believe in as an individual to try anything to harm her. Especially how her contact was an old friend and my old commanding officer from withing the Federation. We flew together, fought together, he knew my family... naturally I don't blame him for being pissed about the possibility. I know who I am, I know what I stand for... and I will be damned if I let anyone call that into speculation.

Taking advantage of the moment... I asked ~~censored~~ about someone who was in fact compromised and trying to influence my way of thinking. She had confirmed she knew something was up but didn't want to upset the friendship... if only there wasn't something nagging at me for some time saying I needed to cut this individual out of my life.

July 13th, 2023

My younger sister ~~censored~~ had a prenatal checkup, to determine the gender of the baby as well as monitor ovarian cysts that tend to run in the women of my family. Much to my sister's disappointment, the doctor confirmed that the baby is likely a girl. Mostly cause, in typical sibling fashion, she didn't want to admit I was right.

Also, the young lady who I likely rescued as a child before coming to Earth, she found old family photos showing the exact dress she was in, helping validate the timeframe of our mutual encounter from before I was "Dakota." It is a bit of a surreal feeling finding these threads to some other life. I wonder if this is how amnesia patients feel?

July 25th, 2023

I woke up from a dream, the last time I saw something with this much detail meant someone was either coming into the world or getting ready to leave. There was a girl, -censored-, I hadn't seen since high school. She looked older, obviously, different hair style but I recognized her right away.

Like something out of a psychic medium TV show, the dream presented itself like it was her spirit trying to reach out after being murdered. I recognize the area as being outside of -censored- in more of a suburban area. She had been messing around with heavy drugs and it ended up getting her killed. I was the one to try finding the body. The body was found in a pile of garbage, near a compound where some major traffickers operated out of. When she was recovered, there was a confrontation.

Apparently the traffickers who killed her were known for taking human remains as trophies. Members had tried intimidating me and showed their collection of severed human heads. Again, this all was in the dream state.

When I woke up, I immediately looked her up. There was too much of a realism to the visuals. It took me a second to remember the last name she was going by. Once I remembered that much, I found public pleas on social media of people asking for prison pen pals to write to ~~censored~~. I dug a bit deeper and found court records involving several drug charges against her since 2016. Her latest mugshot matched how I saw her dead body in the dream almost to a tee. She was due to be released on probation soon, but it's obvious there is a downward spiral in effect.

I am honestly not sure what to do with this one. There are rumors of traffickers in the area connected to Mexican cartel. And it's been so long since she and I saw each other, and her compromised mental state might have erased any memory she had of me. The fact she's been in and out of prison alone may be keeping her from meeting this fate.

August 2nd, 2023

Mass UFO sighting reported to authorities. A triangle craft that was first spotted south of Hollister, just over the Idaho/Nevada line, flew over Twin Falls, then was spotted in Jerome, Shoshone, before possibly being intercepted by other military craft and led towards Sun Valley.. The one news outlet that even mentioned it barely gave it the attention of a passing joke.

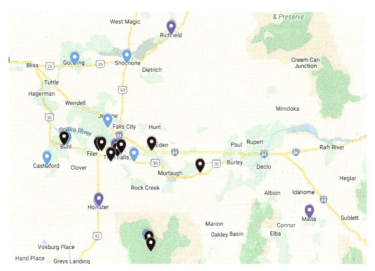

Map of UFO Sightings Near Dakota

Blue - August 2nd Mass Sighting, Black - Dakota's Own Sightings, Purple - Sightings Related to Roswell Incident

I was tipped off by a contact of mine in a local dispatch center after ten calls came in about a strange low-flying craft. I was in close enough proximity to potentially catch a look but could not find an easy escape from my civilian job to do so in time. I had literally just clocked in. The reason it sparked interest was that this was the first time that the dispatch center ever had that many phone calls come in about a low-flying craft. The calls themselves weren't necessarily out of the norm, most of the time they were about people assuming small planes were about to crash, not realizing a small private airstrip was in the area. But numerous people, all calling about the same thing? Between the agencies in the area, about 30 calls were placed

Enough calls came in where I was able to get a solid flight path. Videos backed that something was in the sky that night that hardly made any noise. Flight radars did not show it or the occupying jets. So my contact wouldn't get in too much trouble for discussing work related matters to an outsider, they sent me a link to a Facebook group where the incident was being discussed in real time.

My best evaluation was this was a military test flight. Not uncommon for this time of year. While monitoring the news outlets I also learned that apparently the local military and the Salt Lake branch of the FBI may have had a hand in killing press coverage of UFOs back in the 40s with the Twin Falls Saucer Hoax. The "hoax" was a small 30-inch UFO that was found in someone's backyard and written off as an elaborate prank done by unknown teenagers. This took place roughly three days after the Roswell, New Mexico crash.

August 24th, 2023

At 6:15am this morning I was out walking my cat and noticed an odd light above my house that started to move on its own. I pulled out my phone to record video of the incident and it stayed in view, just inching across the sky. It was solitary, varied in light intensity, and seemed to be flying South by Southwest towards the Nevada line. Strangely enough, it seemed like the object would disappear and reappear at an earlier point in its trajectory multiple times. As the sun rose the object became less visible by comparison, obviously, but still shined bright enough for it to be seen by the naked eye and captured on camera. The incident lasted about 50 minutes before coming to an end.

September 3rd, 2023

An orange light darted through the sky as I was leaving for work. Time was about 7pm... still light outside.

October 19-22, 2023

Earth - United States - Orlando, Florida - GSIC

This is an event I am merely noting to have high potential. A convention is coming together in Orlando, with those who have offered up the most evidence pertaining to my case being in attendance and as speakers. This should get interesting. Some of my communication methods, divination and spirit box based, have also indicated that I may have a surprise waiting for me.

October 19th 2023

I arrive in Orlando after a day of traveling. Seeing ~~censored~~ and hugging her for the first time seemed to trigger flashbacks of the day ~~censored~~ and I rescued her. Possibly an escape pod, or an empty stasis bay... what was that about?

October 20th 2023,

As usual ~~censored~~ triggered flashes, her speech on the Atlantis Resurgence. Did I have something to do with the mass evacuation? Maybe…. During the session with ~~censored~~, she taught the audience how to "reach heaven." Suicide cult jokes aside, the visuals I saw seemed much more intense than other who described their situation. I remember seeing hundreds of children, beautiful landscapes, several other people who weren't at the conference saw me up there. Was I getting an overview of everyone else? Might be. My connections are a bit more involved than most. I do also remember seeing my other grandfather, my dad's father...

~~censored~~ was another fascinating tale. His experience going through 20 and backs, paralleled with abuse, does fit into theories about why my connections are so strong. If he comes up on a panel again I might have to ask if he's found any indicators to watch for on finding these locations.

I'm also seeing overlays of two locations, as if I'm here and in a ship. Messages are coming through, saying at least 15 confirmed ETs are present.

October 21st 2023,

I was visited. My family was here. All four of them. I don't recall the full details but the main image I recall, vividly, was my wife's eyes after we kissed. I was hoping to see them in the flesh, get a family photo, but it seems that is still just a bit out of reach.

~~censored~~ talking about her experiences and book seemed to trigger responses in my mind. As well as ~~censored~~, a man who was (allegedly, for the sake of argument, a man who was physically sent here as a baby). A couple people have noticed my reactions are kicking up and expressed concerns, some taking a religious-esque approach and seemingly ignoring who I am. I'm slowly learning to ignore this, but it is a bit annoying.

~~censored~~, god I love that woman's fire. Gotta get her on a show soon. Anyway, her speech was more aimed towards biblical scripture and pointing out that Yhvh was not the benevolent god people figure him to be. There was some triggers there as well.

October 22nd 2023,

Last night was the disco, and I left because of something nudging me to get away from the scene.

I was taken aboard again. Possible opening directed toward my hotel window. I remember flying with my son, he is definitely like me. I feel there was also something he tried talking to me about, possibly about ~~censored~~... there was also something else that I genuinely can't grasp onto at this time.

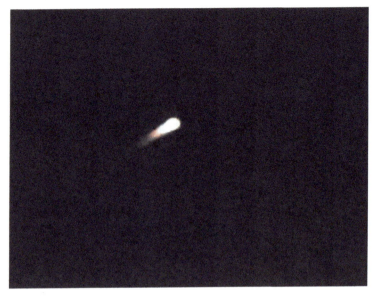

Photo Captured at GSIC of Craft Dakota was Riding

Photo by Tatianna Zalewski

Granted, from our chats I did develop a bit of a crush on ~~censored~~ and as far as things evolving further than friendship is unlikely. Since I deployed I was worried about her, and all the kids I saved and wanted to be able to check in on them somehow. That's all this was, apparently. I still gotta work on my recall. As ~~censored~~ says, it's a constant push that I have to try working at daily.

But it should be noted that when I got up this morning, others at the conference photographed likely craft above the hotel. They saw me!

October 23rd, 2023

The final day of GSIC

~~censored~~ shared their stories of past lives, how they met before, the jobs they completed, and adjusting to how their lives unfolded. A beautiful story of soulmates and overcoming the challenges. ~~censored~~ talked mostly about his background and unveiled a phryll energy device.

With ~~censored~~, I had flashbacks. Some of which included ~~censored~~. I noted having developed a bit of a crush on her and that was part of my influence for choosing to come. Part of what my son wanted to talk about, apparently. There's a guy she linked up with who is... concerning. Part of me wants to write it off as my old habits getting jealous but... I genuinely hope I am wrong. Happy thoughts, happy thoughts. Michael didn't seemed worried, in fact he seemed to like ~~censored~~. But he also noted something... she was not his mother... but she is on Earth and about to make her reveal very soon.

~~censored~~, I, and a few others got together at Outback Steakhouse to have one last dinner together. It was truly great to get connected with them. There was one lady who was there who caught most of our attention, ~~censored~~, who had a very regal presence. The way she would walk, sit, carry herself, you'd expect that to be the behavior of someone from a royalty sort of background. ET? Maybe. It seemed like she may have had a telepathic disposition, and tried getting my attention as such. I'll need to refocus on what happened. I probably should have taken some monoatomic gold. Between that and business cards to accommodate everyone who recognized me.

October 25th, 2023

After a couple days back to civilian life and reflecting on everything that happened, I posted an update video to talk about everything which transpired. When it came to the visit from my son, I started to remember more about what we had talked about.

It seemed that something was bothering him about the missions he had been flying with the GFW, that he was afraid to take them on because of how much he knew that I wanted to see him, his sisters, and his mother. So much so I asked if they would be able to make an appearance. Which, as my previous updates noted, has exactly happened. My son was a bit more vocal, at least as I remember it. Apparently his mind has been partially on edge because he knew of my anticipations for this event, looking forward to potentially seeing them. He expressed his concerns, doing his best to reassure that they did care about me and that, while they would always keep a line open to talk or offer help when it is needed, they are still needed elsewhere to aid in the war.

The Negamuk are now on our side, which was anticipated.

Taalihara will soon be free.

And when I am done with this life.

I'm back in the fight to finish the job…

But this also means that the one person I have been looking for this entire time is in fact on Earth... but where?

November 30th, 2023

There's something I've been wrestling with since GSIC in regards to my memories; and the emotion has only intensified after ~~censored~~ last Star Nation video. It's not anything negative, just overwhelming to say the least. I'm doing my best to swallow my pride and share as I was hoping to get some input. Let's just say, those of you who know about what I've shared in regards to my case, can probably figure this is the only spot I can really share. I'll try to keep it short...

For those who don't know, here's a brief summary:

I'm from Taalihara, went rogue and killed a Ciakharr that was about to eat three kids, joined the GFW as a field medic/scientist after I fled, married a T'Ashkeru woman, had a couple kids, worked with ~~censored~~ on abduction rescues before taking on this envoy deployment.

Elena has personally validated this much, I made sure to check with her once ~~censored~~ came up before I ever said anything publicly. I was able to gather this much from following ~~censored~~ advice on how to handle recalls and dig for more. That and I found one of the kids (obviously now a grown woman) ~~censored~~ and I rescued, even had her on my show, and kept in touch with her to help her out with things she was working on.

The rescue would've taken place in the late 80s, early 90s. Aside from when I had -censored- on the show and it was obvious -censored- tapped in, I hadn't seen much of the guy since then. However, it did seem that during one of -censored- appearances on my show, -censored- pulled out a holographic projection of my wife. That guy knows a bit more than he's letting on... and he seemed to know that I sense it. Oh well, gotta work through the process

I made it a point to go to GSIC because I knew my friend was going to be there. She'd ask if I was going but I didn't want to make any false promises. Obviously I managed to work everything out, and fully intend on making the next one. I also managed to chat with my star family, and while they said they've been busy with some other situations, they would try to make an appearance. Needless to say they kept their word and as amazing as that was, it opened the door to a new "revelation."

When I talked about my abduction when I was six, some suggested that -censored- and I may have had something in common, in that my ending up 30 miles away from home one night might've been an unconscious teleportation episode. As it turns out, you may have been partially correct. I may have found my -censored-...

I'm about 70% certain that not only is my wife on Earth for an envoy deployment. But the thing is, if she is here, her head's either not quite as unlocked or (if I'm reading things right) something's spooking her from digging deeper. The fact that I'm barely turning 28 next month and have as much figured out as I do seems to be an anomaly in itself.

Here's what I know:

After the rescue, ~~censored~~ and I had a one-on-one as he caught me deep in thought. Something about THAT rescue hit harder than the others. There was a brief period where I had time to get my affairs in order before going down for my envoy, so it gave me time to process everything. I told him that I was just thinking about the kids and if I'd get to find them while I was down here. It was then that ~~censored~~ gave me a clue, saying "just remember the moose." He smiled and playfully winked, his way of telling me "hint hint, you already know"

While I've been down here, I've come to realize my kids were the ones to physically come down to Earth to get to me. My wife would always meet us upstairs... as if she can't physically come down out of fear of upsetting something.

There would be several "visits" from my wife that felt more like I was being playing video messages rather than a physical visitation, something akin to the movie Interstellar when Matthew McConaughey's character would watch messages from home.

Working with ~~censored~~, it seems like some rules were bent to give me a jumpstart on realizing I wasn't from Earth. Technically they aren't supposed to as an envoy catching on too early might cause psychological distress. I've come to realize lately that my kids had a hand in it, they found loopholes with me. Why would they do that? If I'm right, they're trying to help mommy and daddy get back together.

Working with ~~censored~~ I've realized that part of why my kids are trying to push things the way they have been is because they knew that I wanted to remember. I wanted it bad enough to help override any "blocks" that were in place early on.

My friend in question, I found her through Tiktok. She would do videos on spiritual, conspiracy, ET sorts of topics and I was quickly impressed by how much work she put into her materials. After a while, I reached out to her through email to ask her for an interview. She was also a fan of ~~censored~~, so yes I did name drop her because ~~censored~~ was scheduled to make an appearance on Bald and Bonkers that weekend. Ironically this was the episode where I asked ~~censored~~ if I was technically having an affair with the ladies I've dated on Earth while I was still technically married upstairs...

While recording her episode, I surprised my friend by using CE5 and a spiritbox to reveal her real name (that she never disclosed on air). This lead her to reveal a possible screen memory, something believed by ET researchers to be a false memory to cover interaction off world.

December 2023 – August 2024

Keeping a record has been challenging with the balance of work, life, and the supernatural—it's quite the juggling act. Yet, the standout moments are transformative. ~~censored~~ welcomed a baby girl into the world, slightly overdue but perfectly healthy. ~~censored~~ In a light-hearted spirit, my mother and grandmother have toyed with the idea of a nickname for her, -censored- , in honor of her birth on Pearl Harbor Remembrance Day.

The most profound discovery, however, was meeting my star wife. The clues were always there, hinting at her earthly presence. Once we had the opportunity to meet and bond, the ensuing experiences have been nothing short of miraculous. We've witnessed unusual phenomena, she's received visits from Elaryon, and even the children confirmed that -censored- is indeed an incarnation of my Iveena. This all came to light during Olivia's wedding, held aboard one of the four GFW motherships orbiting Earth, where she married a Meton male. Michael, though on assignment elsewhere, attended via holographic projection, not wanting to miss his sister's special day.

At the wedding, I found a moment to share a slow dance with Iveena. During our dance, I asked her if the woman who had stepped forward was indeed her earthly representative. Overwhelmed by the emotions of the day, Iveena confirmed it with a nod. That moment of vulnerability gave me a glimpse into her mind, revealing flashes of her

AI Rendering of Dakota and Iveena

life on Earth, including aspects of our current relationship. Some of these memories have already unfolded.

Initially, ~~censored~~ had reservations about the extraterrestrial situation, despite her fascination with the supernatural and an open mind. The idea of having another family somewhere out there can unsettle the most fundamental beliefs about life. I know it did for me when I was just twelve. The realization that she could be the envoy of my celestial spouse brought forth a flood of memories that I'm still trying to process.

It just seems like every moment I have a chance to sit and process something new has come forward. Just establishing an interpersonal connection with *-censored-* has strengthened the connection to the space family. The communications seem much stronger, my astral self has been photographed in a partial manifestation, and even voices can be intercepted via radio transmission interference. On top of somehow getting the affections of a truly beautiful woman I had spent sixteen years trying to find, just for the sake of seeing she is real, the truth about who I am is coming out.

Oh how I could go on and on about this lady, she is truly incredible. Hopefully the promise I made to Olivia to always keep fighting because "Mommy is going to need me to help her," is much more light-hearted in nature than what I feared. ~~censored~~ has shown an immaculate ability to see into the souls and mind's of others, even though she finds herself doubting the legitimacy of what she sees. In some ways this reminds me of times I'd say that my ideal mate would be akin to television series *Ghost Whisperer*. This woman is simply perfect, even if the supernatural circumstances surrounding us hadn't bound our attentions, I firmly believe I'd still fall hard for her.

But now that I think about it, does this technically put us in a bootstrap paradox? Technically the kids, and our other selves, come from a point roughly 300 years into this planet's future. It's probably best not to give it too much thought at this time... it's a bit of a headache. If the vision I saw of me proposing to her in this life comes to fruition... well I'd be the luckiest bastard alive.

Oh yeah, before I get on to other aspects that have come to light, we now have four children starside. Three girls, and a boy... interestingly enough as ~~censored~~ and I were shown the baby, my celestial mother-in-law from Sirius B and our oldest daughter decided to pay the envoy of my star-wife a visit to ensure her health was unaffected. After some discussion ~~censored~~ suggested we call the newest baby Lily.

AI Rendering of Baby Lily

It seems something about how strong our connection is might be cause physical ailments at times... a bit scary to think about. But they ensure everything will pass without incident. Which is probably why it took so long for other aspects of my counterpart's history to come forward.

AI Rendering of Elaryon as WW2 German Solider

Revelations about Elaryon have also come to surface. During his days within the Taal Shiar regime, it appears that my other self was among a group of soldiers sent to infiltrate the Nazi regime. I thought I'd recognized Nazi symbols during recall sessions, but I couldn't believe what I was seeing. On July 1st, ~~censored~~ posted a video in regards to Maria Orsic and how she had been manipulated into providing this planet with blueprints to build sophisticated craft. This insertion, this act of infiltration, would explain why her image triggered recalls of being in a dark room receiving a mission briefing, and us soldiers being told that this woman was used and was to be killed.

Adolf Hitler addressing a rally in Germany, c. 1933.

https://www.britannica.com/event/Nurnberg-Rally#/media/1/407190/84981

The video mentioned ~~censored~~ stating deals were struck between the Taal Shiar and the Third Reich sometime before 1940. What makes this interesting is the fact that I have found two photos (likely more) of Hitler walking the grounds during Nuremberg rallies dated 1927 and 1936 that show an individual who strongly resembles a young Elaryon (one photo shown above, look at the gentleman behind Hitler looking directly at the camera).

The fact the Taal is perhaps the closest related species to humans on this planet, it becomes a bit easier for them to walk among us without being noticed. The fact that apparently Elaryon spent some time on Earth gives me a chance to piece together some truly incredible evidence in a linear timeframe.

But in spite of the tremendous progress made, I have to report one loss. My partner in crime with Bald and Bonkers and I are no more. We had been drifting for some time, coming to blows over how to do the shows, and in private conversations a perceived lack of personal respect and an eagerness to stir drama pushed me over the edge. I'm just done, but I do wish him well in his endeavors. I just wish, with the remaining aspects of kinship I felt when we first became friends, that he'd just be more honest.

The issues started a while ago when I had suspected me was intentionally trying to deceive and manipulate the events surrounding my ET contact, trying to stir me away from those who actually provided useful intel and doubted in sincerity. The moron had no clue I had him under surveillance. A part of me is able to write that off as misunderstanding, until it became obvious that he was once again seeking to boost his own ego under false pretenses and lied to my face when I had the evidence. Maybe in time I'll find the heart to mend that bridge, but it is for the best we go our separate ways.

August 8, 2024

Visit to Dune-like planet, intense battle ensues after greenish blue meteor strikes, invaded by white Terminator robot looking soldiers. I had to have been away for at least two months, in spacetime. In Earth's linear time it might've seemed like only a few minutes. I've really got to sit on this. I released a recording of Intergalactic Gigolo to publicly timestamp this incident until someone within my network potentially comes up with something connected.

Sketch by Dakota of "Dune-Like" Planet, Enhanced by AI

September 2, 2024

On ~~censored~~ YouTube channel, diplomatic relationships involving the ~~censored~~ are discussed. The description of this race definitely seems to be a viable candidate for residing on the Dune-like planet. I've discussed this connection a bit in detail on new segment of Bald and Bonkers I have titled Intergalactic Gigolo. The full listing fo Intergalactic Gigolo episodes can be found: https://youtube.com/playlist?list=PLkDvo91I6DBAlza9moIlrrA-A3fr5RPa_&si=7TRIjq45ZTBI7vBa

September - October, 2024

The final-sih entry for this text...

I am leaving this as a record to let the reader know that this is not the end of the story; much more is continually being uncovered on an almost daily basis and it has been quite difficult for me to simply keep up. There are more entries I will add in time, hopefully making things understandable for the common man. There's also matter to which I am sworn to secrecy until further notice. More interactions with my star family have taken place, including a revelation that my oldest celestial daughter is pregnant at the time of writing this. That's right, I'm going to be a grandfather. I'm not even thirty!

Within the last couple weeks, I have people wanting to loop me back into my bounty hunting days after police raids took place and human remains were found under similar conditions to a case I worked years ago. I've also been on the lookout for an illegal pet kinkajou some asshat abandoned and let run wild, hoping to capture and transport the creature somewhere it can get the proper care before the winter officially hits. By the beginning of October the creature was found, weak from a lack of food but overall healthy.

In the final days of September, I am also trying a little experiment involving an event being hosted down in Colorado to see if my rides with my star family would be seen by more witnesses. So far it seems highly likely, but the exhaustion from me not properly maintaining the exercise regime is leaving me with physical ailments. Nothing that a bit of R&R can't fix. It was organized by ~~*censored*~~ to have multiple craft show up, and my son was one of the pilots. From my count, there were at least fifteen separate craft, some utilizing drones for added effect. I could be misinterpreting what I had seen, I wish I was physically at the location to get a closer look but my priorities have shifted greatly within the last year.

I had heard whispers of a mass sighting arranged, a small cluster of craft and maybe an advanced one from Earth loosely based on ET craft. The infamous TR-3B Antigravity craft to be exact. Officially they don't exist. Here in Idaho I've personally witnessed one, as did hundreds of others in a mass UFO sighting that remained off of news media websites. The main reason I was notified was because of my contacts in local law enforcement.

Back to the event, the remote viewing experiment was a success on my part. Crowds were a bit more... eccentric this time around. Which is good, to an extent, you don't want toxic people ruining the vibe of a major event. It made it somewhat harder to focus, many moving factors at play. During the height of the event I recall being able to see at least 15 craft. The alleged TR-3B looked a bit too "sleek," prompting me to believe it may have been a newer model in the same "family" of craft. I had to withdraw a bit of my efforts as I had developed a migraine from exhaustion... my personal life has been in a bit of chaos. Between rebuilding Bald and Bonkers from the ground up after breaking it off with my old partner, maintaining personal relationships, getting myself back into the field for a number of operations, and even expanding into new avenues... it's safe to say I still have quite a bit of growing up left to do.

I think I might have to end this book with one last section...

October 14th, 2024

As per usual, every time I try to sit down and write out my story in some form something always happens to draw in my attention. Truth be told, I may have to let this particular event slide. In the expanse of space, I have recieved news and can validate the matter with my own eyes, that my daughter Olivia has welcomed her first child into the world. Revealed on an episode of "Intergalactic Gigolo," it's a baby girl named Emily.

Between this and my son being "engaged" to a possible (based on her physical appearance) Zygon woman, who lets me affectionately call her "Viv," the family continues to grow.

I couldn't be more proud of my kids. Ireena is almost a teenager now and baby Lily isn't so much a baby but growing to be a proper young lady. Sure the whole time-travel, being in two people across space at the same time, makes things a bit confusing... but it's all love.

10

Reflections of the Specialist

"At the time and date I am writing this letter, it is almost twenty-two years since I first came face to face with beings not of the world. Measuring from this moment in time, it's just been over sixteen years since I learned I wasn't not alone in this universe. Thirteen since I started to go public. But yet only four to truly acknowledge what I was searching for and only a few months have passed since I found the one person I've been trying to find all along. I'm only twenty-eight years old."

This was from a conversation I had with my girlfriend, the confirmed envoy of my celestial wife Iveena. It stood as a testimony to how much of my life was bound to the supernatural, how much of it encapsulated by trying to understand what was happening to me, but most importantly trying to find a woman I feared would be a delusion of a lost mind. Thankfully, the odds of such a misdirection have been deemed to almost zero, at least from the perspective in which I find myself.

Once, the UFO phenomenon was not something I paid much attention to, but as I've become more open to it, there are still elements that trouble me. This includes the public's ongoing disputes and the quasi-religious beliefs some groups have integrated into their views. A particularly distressing memory for me is how, during my school days, children would use the tale of David and Goliath to provoke me into conflicts because of my height. I've come to realize that I'm not the only one in my family to endure such experiences.

There's a lot I've chosen not to disclose here, partly out of respect for the privacy of others and partly because I was never good at documenting certain life events. There were things I desperately wanted to forget, to escape from, and to cut off all ties with. Surprisingly, engaging with the UFO phenomenon compelled me to confront these parts of my past; it was as if I was learning to shed habits from past lives. The experience was bizarre and overwhelming, and there are no words to fully describe it. For the first time, I felt as if I was turned inside out, compelled to confront the truth staring back at me in the mirror.

There were times I wish I was still "upstairs," as many of my friends/mentors refer to space. Up there I was a warrior and healer, a father to four beautiful children, a lucky bastard of a husband to one of the sexiest women I have ever seen, I had friends... there was mutual love and respect. As

I was getting the finishing touches of this text together... Olivia had a baby girl of her own. I'm now a grandfather as well. Conflict still existed, but it was for purpose of morality rather than personal gain.

Down here? It felt like I was hated by everyone, more of a ghost than the spirits in the night. People, self conscious about their own stature, assumed that because I was bigger and taller than them I constantly looked down on everyone. Being that now I stand at 6'7", it's only in the literal sense because mathematically speaking only 0.01% of people in the United States are taller than me. I was judged by aspects of myself I couldn't change. My own mother and grandmother would threaten to play the victim card and involve police anytime I would be visibly upset just to assert dominance over me. I'll admit I can be an asshole at times, something I've been working on, but as much as I am equally grateful for all they have done to help me get as far as I have in life; having the people you're suppose to trust turn on you like that leaves a mark.

Some will probably try to say that I shouldn't mention that aspect, keep family drama in the family. In some regards they may be right, but acknowledging what had happened and how my own mind managed to interpret it all is a step I have to take to ensure the wounds left over are healed. If by me stepping out and acknowledging these truths manages to help others undergoing similar ordeals, then at least I'd done some good. The suggestions of memory recalls also allowed certain events I repressed to surface; like my own father trying to sexually assault me, other family members making threats of sexual violence, or my stepmother possibly exposing me to LSD at a young age.

I'm not going to waste these pages to air my grievances, further editions of this text that may have updated information just might do that. This is to admit something to myself, perhaps set the record straight. This is to help others who struggled telling their own stories find inspiration to speak out. The extraordinary claims I have made of otherworldly encounters have seeded an assumption that I'm after fame and fortune; that I should allocate my time and resources to Earthly matters rather than give attention to the frequent strangeness in my life. Others assumed I had made no attempts at a normal human life, without having asked any personal questions to determine such conclusions.

I've come to the conclusion, and I'm more than happy to to admit I could be proven wrong, that many have developed this notion that all they see plastered upon a two-dimensional surface is the entire story. Which to me seems... lazy. How can one possibly put everything they went through, their knowledge base, their experiences, their feelings, every asset of the human experience onto a flat surface? Put it all in a YouTube video? A Tiktok video or a tweet? Novels may be one such way, but there is only so much one can put into words. Relying on such examples to formulate the full individual; thoughts, feelings, ideas, wants, needs, desires, and all else that makes up the person.

There are a couple things done in this text that might draw some question from the audience; especially considering how many came to know about me. My censoring

I AM THE SPECIALIST OF THE STRANGE | 261

of names was a choice to respect the privacy of others involved, as finding the time to reach out for proper permissions became a bit of a hassle. It was also a choice to follow my preference to work alone and avoid certain dramas to focus more of my energy at the task at hand, to give more focus to where I felt I could do the most good. Like as much as I shouldn't feel any real responsibility towards helping my sister care for her daughter, me not being a part of that little girl's life just feels wrong... especially with how attached I have become.

The things I managed to do in this life are of my own accord, and while I will always remain eternally grateful for the aid others have provided along the way, I grow tired of the dismissal that certain conclusions are because "they" preached it. I am sovereign in my efforts, open to collaboration, but what you see from me is of my own doing and not from any sort of management.

I chose to follow and study the works of certain individuals because by following their advice, even more extraordinary events transpired convincing me of their legitimacy. Of all the "tests" I managed to compile with my research, they were the ones who passed beyond all expectation. It is only a byproduct of the conversations that transpired I find the honor and privilege to call these people my friends. Indirectly I have referenced their works, mainly in identifying the names of ET species, to give more specification to what sorts of entities I have come across rather than the generic labels such as "Pleiadians," "Arcturians," etc... seen in most new age circles. It just seemed more respectful in that way, and in no way is an attempt to try stealing the material of some of the most intelligent people I know.

I came into this just trying to find my family, to understand what was going on, and maybe help others along the way. Have there been missteps? Absolutely, some where it felt like I slammed my face hard into a brick wall. But these missteps are part of learning. And while I may not necessarily agree with how certain individuals may go about their business and how they present this information... I also had time to interact with them one and one enough to know their reason comes from the heart. If anything, that fact alone matter more than all else.

I say this because while this segment is titled "Reflections" there is a statement I wish to make. Just because you read this book, it does not mean you know the full story. I may, one day down the road, decide to rerelease this text with even more entries added to it that might change the entire narrative. My story is far from over, and choosing to substitute human interaction by scoping what materials I released will only lead to further confusion. Believe me, a part of me still gets a bit twisted with everything that happens.

My next new addition to the collection of books I've written to help make sense of my misadventures will be titled, "FrandsenFiles Compendium" and it will go more in-depth to the research side of various interactions. Theories, discoveries, incident analysis; you name it, hopefully I'll have it. My inclusion of artificial intelligence generated images were strictly for illustrative purposes, though I do plan to revitalize some old ideas in order to create my own AI programs. The beginning stages of these are also underway.

I may run my own company, and obviously have bills to pay, but I am not seeking fame or fortune by my endeavors. Numbers on social media may provide a sense of credibility and unlock new avenues, and I'd be lying if I hadn't gotten overly excited when asked to do interviews and such, but that is not the legacy I want to leave. I do what I do because I enjoy it. I do what I do because it seemed like the best way to help others break out of their shell and share their stories so change could occur. I put myself out there, in the ways I do, because it seemed like the best way to reach others who convinced themselves they are alone... something I know all too much about.

But perhaps that is the main lesson in all this? That we are never truly alone and are capable of so much more. That someone, somewhere, in this infinite fragment of creation is always someone who feels for you, cares for you, wants you to thrive. The day the understanding of what it took, what it takes, for these beings to be in this moment in time with us; will be the day mankind on this Earth will truly have evolved. As for what potential lies in wait?

That's for you to decide. Anyone can give you the information about what is out there in the universe, but what will you do with that information to help others?

The only limitation is imagination.

Links for More Information

Visit the Bald and Bonkers Network LLC website for more information: www.baldandbonkers.net

Follow the Bald and Bonkers Network LLC YouTube channel for videos, shows, music, and more: https://www.youtube.com/@BaldandBonkers

Watch "The Hunt for Olivia: The Paraflixx Cut": https://paraflixx.vhx.tv/videos/the-hunt-for-olivia

Watch "Bonds of Beyond": https://paraflixx.vhx.tv/videos/bondsofbeyond-paraflixx-paranormal-plus

Dakota makes a brief appearance on National Geographic's "Drain the Oceans" Season 2 Episode 11 titled "Secrets of Loch Ness"

Read "Dear Kota: Time to Fess up" to uncover Dakota's first literary attempt to understand his strange life; avaliable in bookstores online

New editions of this text may released in the future giving more details to the incidents described

Be on the lookout for "FrandsenFiles Compendium!"

Dakota Frandsen, also known as the "Specialist of the Strange," is a multimedia creator, paranormal investigator, and the founder of Bald and Bonkers Network LLC. With a lifelong passion for uncovering the mysteries of the supernatural, Dakota has built a career around pushing boundaries and exploring the unknown. His journey started as a teenager with nothing but curiosity and determination, leading him to become a recognized expert in the paranormal and occult communities.

Dakota's work spans across various media, from books and music to podcasts and online courses. As the driving force behind Bald and Bonkers Network LLC, he's dedicated to helping others find their voice, no matter how unconventional, by providing tools and resources for personal storytelling and brand development.

In addition to his paranormal expertise, Dakota is a storyteller at heart. His writing often blends personal experiences, supernatural themes, and introspective letters to his younger self, offering readers a unique glimpse into his world of growth, discovery, and survival.

Dakota also leads projects like **"Why We Are Supernatural,"** a collaborative anthology capturing real stories of supernatural encounters, and runs **Bald and Bonkers Network Academy,** which offers free courses designed to empower entrepreneurs and creatives. His ambition to build a global community of storytellers continues to fuel his ever-growing body of work.

Outside of his professional endeavors, Dakota is deeply passionate about creating content that connects people and inspires them to embrace their own journeys, however strange or mysterious they may seem.

Milton Keynes UK
Ingram Content Group UK Ltd.
UKHW051852281024
450367UK00019B/265